**THE
FAMILY
CREATIVE
WORKSHOP**

Carryalls, Cartoons, Carving, Casting,
Ceramics, Cheeses and Churning,
Christmas Celebrations, Collages and
Assemblages, Colonial Crafts, Colour
Psychology, Confections and
Comfits, Cosmetics.

**Plenary Publications International, Inc.
New York and Amsterdam**

The Project-Evaluation Symbols
appearing in the title heading at
the beginning of each project
have these meanings:

**Estimated time to completion for
an unskilled adult:**

 Hours

 Days

 Weeks

Suggested level of experience:

 Child alone

 Supervised child
or family project

 Unskilled adult

 Specialized prior training

Tools and equipment:

 Small hand tools

 Large hand
and household tools

 Specialized
or powered equipment

Publishers
Plenary Publications International,
Incorporated, New York.

Allen Davenport Bragdon, Editor-in-
Chief and Publisher.

Nancy Jackson, Administrative Asst.
Evelyn Kieran, Production Editor.

For this volume
Contributing editors:
Sally Foy, Lady Pamela Harlech,
Anne Masters.

Acknowledgements:
Mosaic of the Emperor
Justinian, courtesy
Scala New York/Florence.

On the cover:
Clay tiles are rolled, cut, glazed and decorated to your
own specifications before firing them for strength and
durability. See "Ceramics", in this volume.
Photograph by Paul Levin.

ISBN 0 7054 0333 5

Filmsetting by C. E. Dawkins (Typesetters) Ltd.,
London, SE1 1UN.
Printed in Holland by Smeets Lithographers, Weert.
Bound by Proost en Brandt N.V., Amsterdam.

Contents

CARRYALLS
Totes and Bags to make

by John Brucciani

The carryall is a symbol of our age. We live at an accelerated pace and are on the move more than we ever were in earlier years. Because we are so mobile, we are almost always in need of an efficient, comfortable container for our belongings. Leather, canvas, and vinyl carryalls fill this need admirably.

Of the three materials, leather is the sturdiest. Because it has no weave, it withstands maximum stress. Canvas has proved its resistance to rough wear through years of sailing applications. Vinyl is a modern, pliable plastic. Clear vinyl tears easily, but when bonded to a layer of foam or cloth backing, it becomes quite sturdy. An advantage of vinyl is that it can be kept clean simply by wiping it with soap and water. Leather has a porous surface, which must be periodically cleaned and oiled. Canvas needs to be washed by machine fairly frequently.

The tote bag, back pack, duffel bag and holdall described on the following pages can be made with leather, canvas, or vinyl. I have made the tote of vinyl, the back pack of canvas, and the duffel bag and holdall of leather, so techniques for working with each of these materials are described on the following pages. You can, using the patterns and instructions for a project—the tote bag, for instance—make that carryall from either of the other two materials.

Special tools for working with leather and leather-like materials are shown in the Craftnotes section, page 16, with detailed drawings of leather working techniques useful for the projects in which leather or vinyl is used. A careful study of the Craftnotes before you undertake vinyl or leather projects is recommended.

Canvas and vinyl can be purchased in many fabric shops. They are sold in a variety of weights, textures, and colours. Leather can be ordered from a tanner or purchased from a commercial leather shop.

Tools and Materials

In addition to the leather, canvas, or vinyl, the basic tools and materials you will need for these projects include the following items:

Pattern-making Paper: Brown wrapping paper is a good substitute.

Masking Tape: For securing patterns to leather, canvas, or vinyl. Cellophane tape will also work.

Shears: A good, sharp pair for clean cutting.

Straight-edge: A metal ruler for measuring and for exact marking of pattern. Wooden rulers are easily displaced as you work and can result in lines which are not straight.

Wax Crayon: For tracing patterns on vinyl surfaces. Or use tailor's chalk.

Rubber Cement: For temporary "tacking" prior to sewing.

Awl: For puncturing holes in leather. It should be quite sharp. A carpenter's awl works well.

Hammer or Mallet: For flattening seams in vinyl and leather. I often use a cobbler's hammer, because it works well for me; but any type of round-headed hammer will do. A really new metal hammer, used too vigorously, could mark leather and should be covered with a couple of thicknesses of nylon or cheesecloth to soften its hitting surface.

A back pack is one of the most useful of modern totes. Made of durable canvas, it will last through a lifetime of travel and is surprisingly easy to make. Instructions for making this one begin on page 11. It can also be made of leather.

Needlecrafts
Vinyl Tote Bag

To make the vinyl tote bag pictured on the facing page, you will need a piece of cloth-backed, medium-weight vinyl 50 by 90 cm, a size 14/90 needle for your sewing machine, and heavy mercerised thread.

Enlarge and cut out pattern pieces, figure B; cut two handles. With masking tape, secure pattern to the wrong side (back) of vinyl; with wax crayon, trace pattern, and transfer all pattern markings. Cut along solid cutting lines of pattern. Set stitch-length selector of your sewing machine at 8 or 10, and test stitch two layers of scrap vinyl to adjust thread tension on the machine. (You can also hand-sew the tote, using heavy mercerised thread smoothed with beeswax and a large embroidery needle.)

Cut out triangles at the base of the tote as shown in photograph 2, and glue and fold top edges together as in photographs 3 and 4.

Figure A: With tailor's chalk or wax pencil, transfer markings from pattern, figure B, to vinyl. This detail shows a square with an X, which indicates sewing lines for joining handle end to bag.

1: A straight-edge ruler is used in drawing a pattern precisely on vinyl. Be sure the work is well lighted, especially when you are making small adjustments.

2: Cut in on the lines that form the triangles at the base of the tote. Remove these two triangles of vinyl. The flaps will later be hand-sewn to the outside of the tote bottom.

3: With a brush, apply a coat of rubber cement to top 10 cm of the bag on the wrong (back) side. Let rubber cement dry completely (about a minute) so surfaces will adhere firmly when pressed together.

4: Fold top 5 cm over on to bottom 5 cm of rubber-cement-coated vinyl, wrong sides together. Press down firmly along fold line for top of tote. This makes a finished top edge for the bag.

This versatile tote bag is made of vinyl, cut as a single piece and glued and stitched in a very simple operation. You can also make it of leather or canvas.

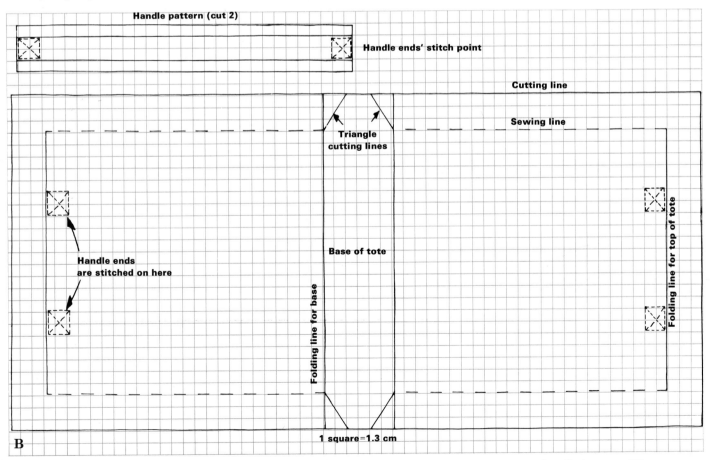

Handle pattern (cut 2)

Handle ends' stitch point

Cutting line

Sewing line

Triangle cutting lines

Base of tote

Handle ends are stitched on here

Folding line for base

Folding line for top of tote

1 square = 1.3 cm

B

Figure B: Tote-bag pattern. To enlarge, for each square draw 1.3 cm square on pattern paper, as described on page 127.

Joining the tote sides

Fold tote so right (face) sides are together, and align glued edges. On the wrong side, stitch the seam along the dotted sewing lines on the pattern from the top of one glued edge to a few stitches short of the bottom corner (see photograph 5). Stitch other side the same way. Leave long threads at seam ends; pull them to inside of the bag; knot two or three times; cut off.

Turn the bag right side out. With heavy mercerised thread, beeswaxed, and a large embroidery or leatherworking needle (see Craftnotes, page 16), hand tack both corners. Be sure corner-flap triangle is on the outside (photograph 6). At last stitch, push needle to inside; pull thread through.

With needle and thread inside, turn the bag inside out; take three stitches on the same spot to secure the thread; then cut it.

Attaching the handles

Follow these instructions for making and attaching each handle:

With handle piece right (face) side down on your worktable, brush entire surface with a light coat of rubber cement, and let it dry completely.

Along fold lines indicated on pattern, figure B, page 9, fold side edges inwards. They should meet in the centre to give handles a neat finish. Press down firmly to flatten glued pieces. Handle is now ready to be attached.

Handle ends are attached by stitching a square and an X within it, as in figures A and B, pages 8 and 9. Match squares and X's of handle end and bag; then place the seamed (wrong side) of handle end to the X'd square on the right (face) side of bag, and stitch a large X in the square at this place (photograph 8). Making sure the handle is not twisted, attach the other end to the same side of the bag, at the other point marked with an X'd square.

Attach the second handle to the other side of the bag the same way.

5: Stitch the side seams together with a sewing machine. Use a seam guide to keep a uniform seam width as you sew. Sew at a slow pace to avoid pulling the vinyl.

6: Hand tack the bottom seam with the tote right side out and the flaps on the outside. Use double thread. Pull needle through with pliers if necessary.

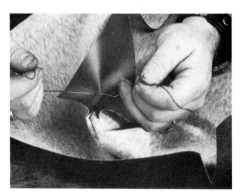

7: Finish hand-stitching with tote turned inside out and triangle flaps still on outside. Tie two or three firm knots; then snip off thread close to the vinyl.

8: Attach handles to sides of tote. When stitching is finished at each end, leave long threads, and pull these through to inside of tote. Knot thread; trim excess.

Needlecrafts
Canvas Back Pack

by Consuela English
This canvas back pack, pictured on page 7 and below, right, uses the basic techniques described in the previous section. It is roomier than the tote, and the large flap protects its contents. You will need 115 cm of 90 cm wide, medium-weight canvas and a heavy-duty snap or buckle fastener. Test your machine to make sure it can handle heavy canvas. Adjust and test stitch length and thread tension as for vinyl. Always iron along fold lines before you start sewing.

Follow procedures in preceding section to prepare the pattern and cut out fabric. Cut two pieces of both strap and back-pack side patterns. Adjust strap length to suit your size—shorten or lengthen if necessary.

Fold, press, then sew straps along dotted lines. Attach straps at X'd squares on strap ends to X'd squares on back-pack pattern, as in preceding section and photograph 9. Fold, press, then stitch flap edges at top of back pack along inner solid line. Tie off threads.

Match dots on side pieces to dots on back-pack pattern. On wrong side, stitch panel to pack from dot to dot. Then continue stitching side piece to pack along seam lines, to right and to left of dots, until three edges are joined. Join second side piece the same way. Then, with the inside out, top stitch all seams.

Attach buckle or snap to flap edge and to pack. Then trim threads and any excess length on the straps, as shown in photograph 10.

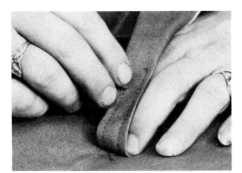

9: Place X'd square on strap end over X'd square on canvas. Machine stitch to join.

10: A neat appearance results from careful trimming of straps and threads.

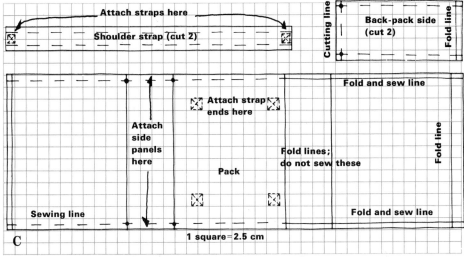

Figure C: Pattern for back pack

(Pattern labels: Attach straps here; Shoulder strap (cut 2); Cutting line; Back-pack side (cut 2); Fold line; Attach strap ends here; Attach side panels here; Fold and sew line; Pack; Fold lines; do not sew these; Fold line; Sewing line; Fold and sew line; 1 square = 2.5 cm; C)

Back pack, popular teen carryall, is made from tough canvas. Books and clothing can be easily carried inside, and hands are left free.

11: Trace cardboard pattern pieces on back of leather. Start by pencilling key line for main pattern piece; then tape down, and trace the pattern.

12: Put rubber cement on right (smooth) side along stitching line at one end of tote and on wrong side at the other end. Let dry. Press ends together. Stitch.

13: Flattening opened-out, glued-down, seam-allowance edges with a hammer. You can use a cobbler's hammer, as here, or a wooden mallet.

▶ Duffel bags can be used to hold everything from groceries to clothes. Made of durable leather, this one will withstand years of rough wear and tear.

Leathercrafts
Duffel Bag

To make this useful duffel bag, you will need 51 by 84 cm of chrome-tanned, lightweight garment leather, four medium-size rivets with 6 mm posts, five brass rings of 2.5 cm diameter, a brass dog-lead clasp, four-ply nylon thread, and, if you are sewing by machine, a heavy-duty needle. If you are hand-sewing, use one of the needles shown in the Craftnotes, page 16, and the same weight thread, coated with beeswax. Or hand lace with 3 mm leather thong, as instructed in the Craftnotes.

On cardboard, enlarge the three pattern pieces, figure D, page 14. Use shears to cut out one of each of the pattern pieces.

Place the cardboard pattern pieces on the wrong side of the leather, as shown in photograph 11. Hold them in place with tape, and trace around them with wax pencil. Cut cleanly with sharp shears.

Apply rubber cement to both sides of bag, as shown in photograph 12. When cement is dry, press together to hold for stitching.

Stitch this seam, by hand or by machine. If you are using a machine, sew

14: Brush rubber cement on face (right) side of the bottom circle. Cement must be evenly distributed all around the edge of the circle, in a band 1.3 cm wide.

15: With the cylindrical bag inside out, press the bottom piece firmly to the rubber-cemented bottom edge of the right side of the cylinder.

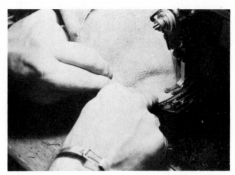

16: Stitch glued circular seam, as close to the edge as possible. If you prefer to make this seam with leather lacing, refer to Craftnotes, page 16.

17: Pound the sides of the shoulder strap flat, with a hammer, after rubber cement has dried. The strap should now be about 2.5 cm wide and quite flexible.

18: Pull one end of the shoulder strap through the ring of dog-lead clasp. Only 2.5 cm of the strap should loop through. The end will be secured with two rivets.

19: Hammer rivets to close strap end around the clasp. Rivet holes can be made with awl and hammer, or a rotary-wheel punch (see Craftnotes, page 16).

very slowly to avoid damaging the leather. If necessary, turn the motor wheel by hand to control the speed of the machine. You now have a cylinder.

Open the seam allowance flat by pulling edges apart. Apply rubber cement to undersides of seam-allowance edges and to leather directly beneath them. Let dry. Press down, and flatten with a hammer, as shown in photograph 13. See also Craftnotes, page 16, for details of this step.

Apply rubber cement to the edge of the circular bottom piece, as shown in photograph 14. Then apply 1.3 cm band of rubber cement to the bottom edge of the right side of the now-cylindrical piece. Let dry. Press cemented edges together, as shown in photograph 15. Stitch this seam by hand or by machine (photograph 16). Finish the top edge of the cylinder by turning down 2.5 cm along fold line and stitching.

Brush cement over the wrong side of the strap piece. Turn both sides of strap piece in to the middle, along fold lines. Press; let dry; pound flat, as in photograph 17. Pull one strap end through the ring of the dog-lead clasp (photograph 18). Make a loop, and fasten loop with two rivets.

With a rotary-wheel punch or an awl, punch four holes, marked on pattern piece, at top of bag; put brass rings through these holes (see photographs 20 and 21, page 14). With an awl and a hammer, make two holes, as noted on pattern, near the bag's bottom, close to the seam. Make first hole; fold fabric in half, along seam; place awl through first hole, and hammer it through the other side. Put a brass ring through both holes. Loop free end of strap through bottom brass ring. See photographs 22 and 23, page 14.

Attach the dog-lead clasp to the five brass rings at the top of the bag to close it, as shown in photograph 24, page 14.

20: With rotary-wheel punch, make four equidistant holes around the top of bag. Awl and mallet can be used instead.

21: Place brass rings through holes. When rings are in place, tighten them securely with pliers.

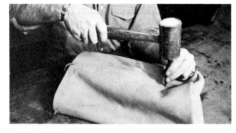

22: Make holes for ring near bottom of bag, using awl and mallet or hammer. Wood block inside protects other side.

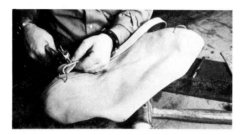

23: Use rotary-wheel punch to make holes for rivets on bottom of the strap, after strap has been closed around ring.

24: To close the duffel bag, snap the dog-lead clasp through the four brass rings at the top of the bag.

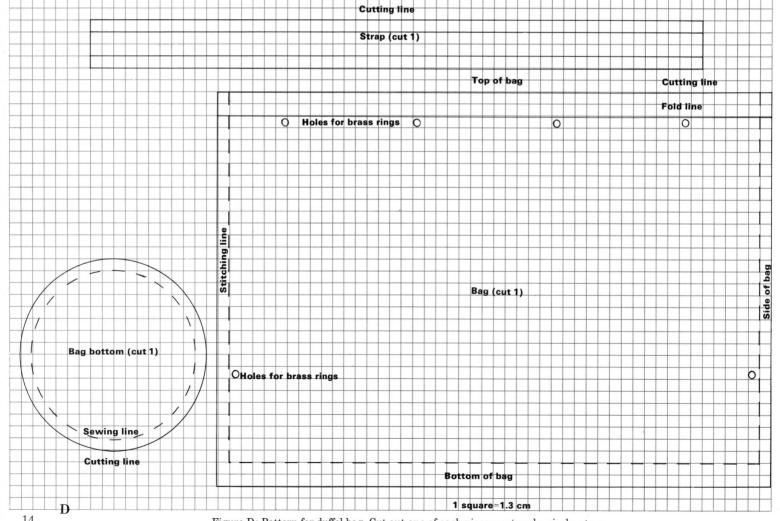

Figure D: Pattern for duffel bag. Cut out one of each piece: rectangle, circle, strap.

Holdall

This holdall bag is a variation of the duffel bag. Use pattern, figure E. You need a piece of leather 66 by 140 cm. Follow instructions for previous projects, with these differences: leave a 33 cm opening between dots on pattern in centre of side seam. Using backstitch, attach 33 cm zip. See the Craftnotes, page 17.

Attach the second circle at the other end of the cylinder. Add two leather handles at X'd squares, one on each side of zip.

25: Zip is sewn into 33 cm opening left between dots on seam allowance (broken line of pattern). Before stitching, glue down seam allowances of zip opening, and tape zip into place, as shown in Craftnotes, page 17.

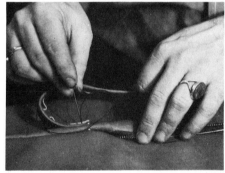

26: Attach handles to the bag, one on each side of the zip opening at the squares marked with Xs. These may be hand or machine stitched. Be sure that the stitching is well done and the handles are firmly attached.

The holdall is a welcome companion on any short trip. It is made much the same as the duffel bag, but is closed at both ends and has a side zip and two straps.

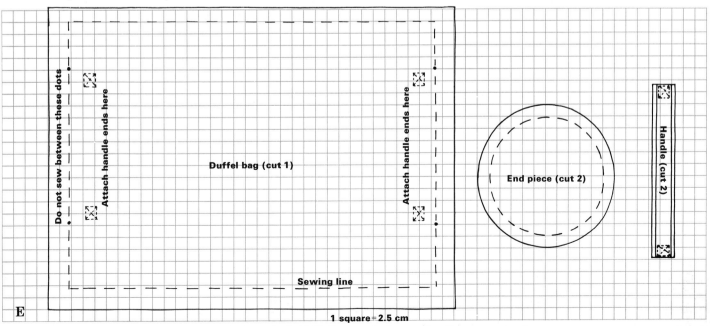

Do not sew between these dots

Attach handle ends here

Duffel bag (cut 1)

Attach handle ends here

End piece (cut 2)

Handle (cut 2)

Sewing line

E

1 square = 2.5 cm

Figure E: Pattern for holdall. Cut two circles, two handles, one rectangle.

LEATHER

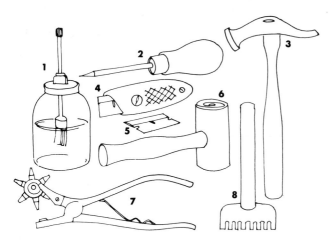

Leathercrafter's basic tool kit: (1) rubber-cement jar with brush; (2) awl; (3) cobbler's hammer; (4) straight-edge craft knife; (5) single-edge razor blade; (6) shoemaker's leather or rubber mallet; (7) rotary leather punch; (8) thonging chisel. Mallet, rotary leather punch, and thonging chisel can be purchased in craft shops and are usually available where leather supplies are sold.

Most common leather-lacing needles, below, left to right: glover's needle, hook-and-eye needle, two-prong split needle, upholsterer's needle. The glover's needle is triangular in cross section, as magnified detail shows. Very sharp, it is used for sewing through leather without first punching holes. The other three needles are for lacing through holes. Lacing can be threaded through the hook-and-eye needle, whereas the two-prong split needle merely grips the end of lacing. Upholsterer's needle aids in sewing hard-to-get-at corners.

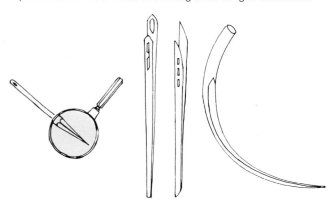

Hints on leather lacing: To lace a leather seam without a glover's needle (right) make holes in the leather large enough to accommodate lacing. The rotary leather punch makes one hole at a time. Select hole size; insert leather; squeeze handle. Space holes evenly over seam line.

The thonging chisel makes a series of small, evenly spaced slits and may be used as an alternative to the rotary punch. Place point of chisel on face side of leather. With a mallet, pound chisel into leather until slit is made. Continue along seam line until you have an evenly spaced line of small slits. Then stitch seam, passing lacing through holes (or slits) as shown in diagrams on opposite page.

When seam is sewn and ends of lacing are secured, sides of seam may be pounded flat with a mallet. Follow instructions and drawings on the opposite page.

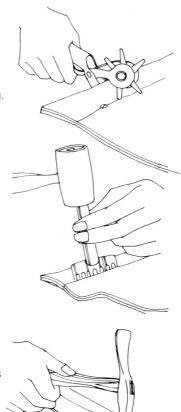

Pounding leather seams: Once you have sewn a seam in leather, you must flatten its sides. Working on the wrong side, open leather along seam line; pound flat with a heavy mallet. Apply an even coat of rubber cement to underside of seam allowances and corresponding areas on leather under seam allowances. Let rubber cement dry for one minute before you press these down. Then ease seam allowances down on to leather beneath, smoothing out bumps with your fingers. Use the cobbler's hammer to pound seam allowances firmly into place. If you work slowly and use even pressure, sides will be evenly flattened.

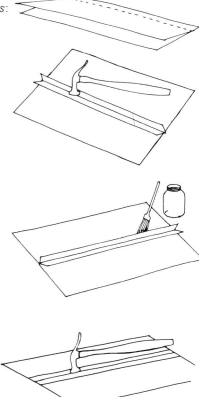

CRAFTNOTES

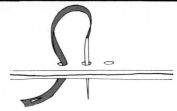

Sewing with Leather Lacing: Cut lacing 15 cm longer than seam. Make a small slit in one end. Thread other end. Bring needle up through first hole from wrong side; insert through second hole.

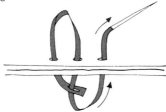

Put the needle through the slit at end of lace, and come up through the next hole.

Continue stitching through holes. Be sure lacing does not get twisted. Do not pull so tight that leather puckers.

To make the last stitch, pull needle down through last hole, or make one more hole so needle ends on the wrong side.

Secure this last stitch by slipping the needle under the previous stitches made on the underside of the seam.

When you pull lacing through last stitch, tug to lock it in. Cut off excess, leaving a tail to prevent its slipping back.

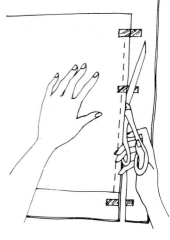

Cutting leather to patterns: The easiest way to cut leather accurately is to follow a cardboard pattern, held in place with masking or cellophane tape. Simply tape cardboard to leather so it is secure. Then, with sharp shears, cut along edge of cardboard pattern, cutting through the tape as you go. . . Use your free hand to keep the pattern in the right position on the leather as you continue cutting. Never pin patterns to leather.

Holding seams for sewing: To hold two matching edges of leather firmly together while you sew, use rubber cement, or hold them with masking tape placed at 4 cm intervals. Stitch over tape; remove it later.

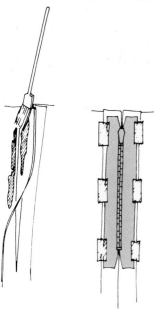

Sewing a zip on to leather: Fold back the seam allowances for the zip opening, and brush the undersides and the surface just beneath with rubber cement, as shown in the sketch at left. When the rubber cement has dried, in about 60 seconds, press the cement-covered surfaces together, and hammer them flat. Fasten the zip in place face down with tapes as shown in sketch at right. Stitch zip into place, then remove tapes.

CARTOONS

Say it with a Smile

by Ray Gill

Cartoon drawing is telling stories in pictures. Its earliest beginnings were the cave drawings of prehistoric man. Primitive societies used picture stories as a method of communication, as well as a magic performed to bring good fortune. About 20,000 years B.C., Cro-Magnon man made coloured cave drawings similar to the drawings below.

Each era, Egyptian, Greek, medieval, Renaissance, produced its own art, always with the same story-telling quality. Line drawing, so much like today's cartoons, was etched, painted, carved, and lithographed.

Cartoonist Ray Gill, on these two pages interprets cartoon history, from cave art, below, and political cartoons, opposite page, to the comics which are depicted as Gill's own style across the bottom of these two pages.

Cave drawings, represented here, are among the earliest records of story-telling pictures.

Drawings that satirized politics eventually led to single-panel and strip cartoons all peopled by figures everyone could laugh at and identify with.

The word cartoon was first applied to the full-size design or sketch for an oil painting, tapestry, or mosaic. The word acquired its present meaning by accident. In 1841, when both the Palace of Westminster (where the Houses of Parliament convene) and the humorous weekly *Punch* were in their beginnings, Prince Albert commissioned designs for frescoes to adorn the walls of the new palace. Some of them were so bad that *Punch* reproduced the cartoons for the designs and captioned them satirically. The *Punch* cartoon was born, and the word acquired its new meaning.

Caricature and satire combined with line drawing grew to be a powerful weapon, socially and politically. The political cartoon has long been recognized as a force to be respected. Editorials may or may not be read and understood, but almost everyone understands cartoons, and they have brought about both social and political change.

Publications such as *The New Yorker* popularized single panel cartoons with one-line captions. Sometimes not even the one line was needed. Earlier, the comic strip was created. The "Yellow Kid", by Richard F. Outcault, so called because it was overprinted with yellow, was first published by the New York *World*. It was recognized as a winner by William Randolph Hearst, who enticed Outcault to his New York *Journal*. The *World* brought him back. In the ensuing controversy, the term 'yellow journalism' was born, and so were coloured comics. Syndication of comic strips led to their appearance in papers around the world. Then came the comic magazine.

This is a take-off on drawings typical of the weekly magazine *Punch*, which were the forerunners of modern comic strips.

Heroes of strip cartooning, like "Dagwood Bumstead", shown in Ray Gill's interpretation, proliferated and evolved into superheroes such as the "Flash Gordon" type. More recently anti-heroes, such as "Fritz the Cat", rival Flash Gordon in popularity.

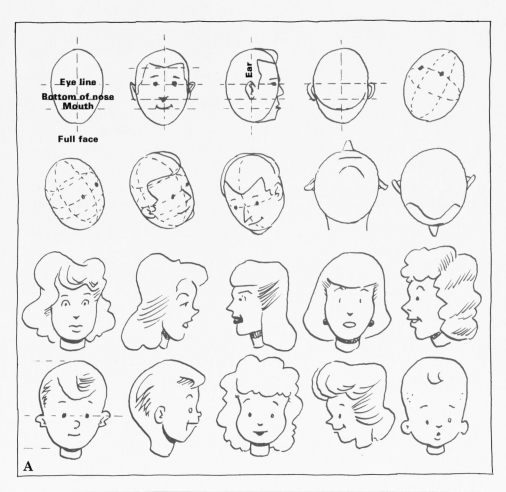

Figure A: Sketches on the right illustrate the basic oval used in cartoons to represent the human head, and show how the angle of the oval, and lines added to the oval, can create cartoon representations of the faces of men, women, and children. These simplified faces acquire depth and life by the addition of pencil shading in the three sketches above. Working with a blown-out egg-shell supported by an egg-cup, you can develop a feeling for the shape the oval assumes from various angles. Dotted lines show how relative positions of features remain unchanged even when angle at which the head is seen does change. Hairline is added after the features have been positioned and does much, as you can see in figures A and B, to characterize the person as man, older man, woman, child.

Graphic Arts
Heads, Faces, Expressions

Acquiring a cartoon technique and using it with kindness can add more to daily family and community life than you might suppose. A cartoon congratulating a child on a scholastic feat or a sports success means more to him than would a simple verbal O.K. A cartoon view of a family problem or chore to come can express it without sting. You can also use cartoon techniques to dramatize community messages and advertise projects.

Do not be put off by the notion that you do not have artistic talent. Cartoons can be put together in a fairly mechanical way, once you know how.

Choose a style that suits you

There are many kinds of cartoons to experiment with, and one of these will probably seem easier than others. The simplest is the single-panel cartoon (see pages 24 and 25), whose function is to illustrate a joke, which may or may not be expressed with a caption below. Once you have learned how to make a single panel cartoon character, you can trace and cut out your character, pin his arms, legs, and head together with drawing pins, fix him to your drawing paper, and trace him in the various actions needed to illustrate a panel or even a panel series.

Or you can scribble a doodle, like those on pages 28 and 29, and from the basic forms evolved create characters that illustrate a single-panel cartoon or a strip or a story.

Since all cartoons start with one or more main characters, drawing these characters is the first technique to acquire. The head and facial expression are the most important elements in these figures.

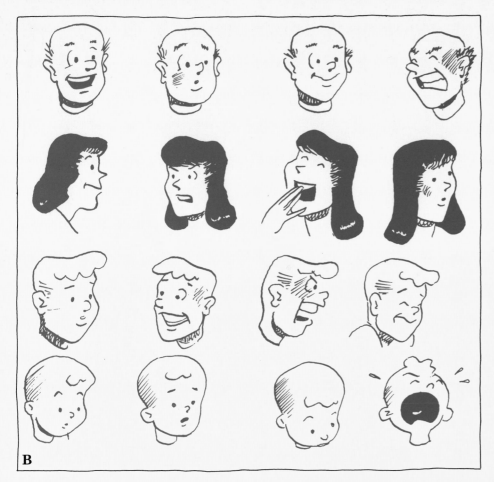

B

Figure B: Sketches above and on the left show vivid facial expressions created by pencil lines on the basic oval faces illustrated on the opposite page. By studying the drawings, you can see how simply you can portray emotions. A good technique for mastering the drawing of facial expressions is to look in a mirror and make faces at yourself—really let yourself go. Exaggerate your features for comic effect. Study the faces of your friends, and try to discover mannerisms and characteristics that you can turn to good comic use. Remember that, to an aspiring cartoonist, the whole world is a classroom.

For drawing purposes, the human head is egg shaped, as in figure A. Full face, eye line is about halfway between head top and chin. Hair is not included in relative position of features. Bottom of the nose is half way between eye line and bottom of the chin, mouth about half way between nose and chin. A child's eye line is lower than an adult's; but nose and mouth distances are the same. The lower the eye line, the younger the child. These measurements are simplified but practical. Try them, and adjust them to suit yourself. For a profile, the ear is drawn in the centre. Its top is even with the eye line; its bottom lines up with bottom of the nose.

Start with egg-shell models

To get started on drawing heads, make some models. Empty and clean three eggs. Pierce each end with a large darning needle, and stir the contents. Take a deep breath, and blow the egg out of the shell. Turn one egg large end down for a man, two eggs small end down for a woman and a child. Place the eggs in eggcups so they will stand upright. With a felt marker, draw dotted lines to locate features, as in figure A. Turn the eggs so the faces look up, down, or to the side. Continue to use these models to sketch from until you feel you are proficient enough to work without them.

Before trying to draw an expression, feel the emotion yourself. The cartoonist is writer, director, cameraman, and actor. See the sketches above for simple ways to indicate feelings. Curve the mouth up for a smile, down for anger. Look in a mirror and make your face show the feeling you want to portray. Then draw it.

You will discover that you have natural acting ability and that your expressions can be interpreted in terms of lines. Your drawing style will be personal. Start with ordinary paper and a soft pencil. Then graduate to a medium-size black felt pen and white board.

Figure C: This simple model, made of corks and pipe cleaners, with modelling clay for a base, will be a big help when you are learning to draw the human figure. Bend it into different positions, and sketch it from several angles.

C

▶ Figure D: Two paper cut-out puppets are useful aids. One represents a boy, and the other, almost identical but smaller, a girl. Trace them, cut them out of cardboard, pin them in poses, as shown, and draw from them.

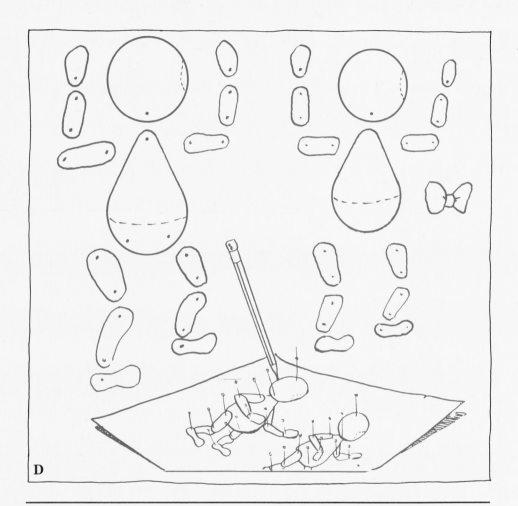

D

Graphic Arts
Drawing Figures and Hands

The best way to learn to draw the human figure is by sketching from life. There are other ways, and two are illustrated in figures C and D.

If you have, or can buy, an artist's model, a figure with moveable limbs, you can pose it in any action and sketch from it. You can make a simplified version of an artist's model as shown in figure C. Use different sizes of corks for head, chest, and hips, and connect them with sections of thick pipe cleaners. Pipe cleaners make the arms and legs. A lump of modelling clay serves as a base. Extensions from bottoms of the heels stuck into the clay hold the figure upright. Bend the pipe cleaner limbs and spine to achieve any pose you want.

Or trace the disjointed figures in figure D; transfer them to cardboard, and cut them out. Tape down the corners of the board you are going to draw on, so it will not move about. Lay the figures (one is for a small boy, one for a small girl) on the board; position them for the action, and pin to the board. Pin the pieces together with dressmaker's pins, one at each joint plus any needed to hold the figures in place. Trace around the figures in pencil, and then remove them.

I developed these figures into characters for a daily single-panel cartoon called "Adam 'n Evie". Samples of this feature are shown on pages 24 and 25. Study them, and use them as a reference.

Balance is the key to making an action look right. If the top of the figure bends forwards, the middle must bend backwards for balance. If the figure is walking, moving ahead, it must lean forwards a bit. Action is achieved by drawing in balance. Study other cartoons to learn how they were done.

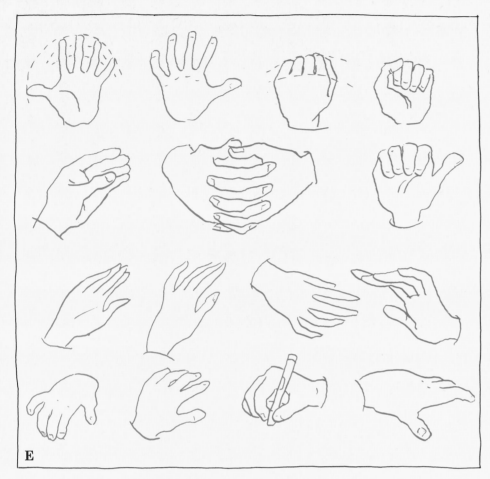

E

Figure E: Sketches on the left show how hands of men, women, and children differ. Look at the second row in the figure. A man's hands tend to be massive and powerful. The fingers of a woman's hands, third row, are slender and tapering. The hands of a child have a soft, chubby look, as in the fourth row. Hands can be extremely effective in conveying expression. Pose and observe your own hands, and draw from them. Also, keep an eye on other people's hands, and watch how they hold and move them. Hand above, indicating direction, suggests one way hands can be used in cartoons to "talk".

How to draw hands

Hands are the hardest part of the body to draw in cartoons. Treat them mechanically at first. Simplify them. Or have your cartoon characters wear mittens, if you find this necessary.

Eventually, however, most cartoonists face the fact that a hand has four fingers and a thumb, and they draw them. So that you will make the hands in proper proportion to the figure, remember that an open hand is about the size of a face and that palm breadth is about the same as the distance from bottom of nose to tip of chin. It is also helpful to think of a hand as a square block. Get the block in perspective, and the fingers and thumb will fit on nicely. If you go at it as if the hand were an octopus, that is exactly what it will look like when you draw it.

Learn from your own hands

Pose one hand doing an action, and draw what you see. Then copy the hands in figure E. Correct what you have drawn. The result should be pretty good.

Women's hands are more graceful and slender than most men's hands. The little finger juts out; the thumb is held close to the palm; the hand may hang limply from the wrist. Draw these hands with a smooth line rather than an angular line, and they will look feminine.

Children's hands are smaller, fingers and thumb shorter and pudgier. Like women's hands, they are graceful, however, and display similar elements, such as extended little fingers and tentative gentleness—think of a child's hands holding a butterfly. Again, sketch from life whenever possible. A trick: Draw the main action line of a child's hands quickly; then add the rest. This technique is also good for sketching animals. Children and animals move too fast for a studied portrait. Finally, realize that hands usually play a big part in conveying expression. Try to capture this function.

Graphic Arts
Single-panel Cartoons

Heads, faces, expressions, figures are the basic elements in the simplest of all cartoons, the single panel joke. The other elements are the accessories that surround the main figures, the background or setting, and the caption.

By accessories to the main figures, I mean the pirate ship, for instance, in the cartoon on the left and the naïve toys held by Adam 'n Evie. The pirate ship sets the reader up—prepares him—for the caption. The toys emphasize the innocence of the children and counterpoint their would-be-mature interpretations of the world.

Use Adam 'n Evie to evolve single panel cartoons of your own. The basic shapes that compose the youngsters are two circles, one for the head, one for the hips, and a cone shape for the chest area. Using circles and cone shapes, you can create other accessories and characters as needed: toys, adults, or, perhaps, a big dog, which can pull Adam on his wagon, lick his face, eat his ice-cream cone when Adam is not looking.

The setting for your cartoons will require drawing some form of background. The easiest background is a natural, slightly curved, horizon line, with a bit of foliage for decoration, as in the cowboy cartoon, left. A few simple lines can indicate a fence and pavement, as in the cartoon on the opposite page. But to draw background properly, you must understand a bit about drawing in perspective. To simplify this, think about looking down a railway track, and remember how the rails seem to come together when they reach the horizon. This is called the vanishing point. This visual principle makes objects appear smaller in the distance. Dark objects appear to be lighter. To use this principle in cartoons, study figure F. and note how all the lines in this one-point-perspective drawing converge. I used Evie's eye line to determine the point of convergence. I stuck a pin in the board at

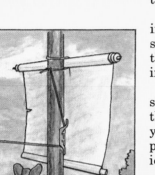

"I suppose they had pirates so they'd have something to think about on those long, dull voyages over the empty seas."

"Hey, do they call this a revolver because they start revolutions with it?"

"I can't understand some people. They keep saying to me, 'Isn't he wonderful for his age.' But they say the same thing about Grandpa, and he's an awful lot older than me."

this point, placed a ruler against the bottom of the pin and across the drawing, and drew the dotted line. This gave me the perspective for the face and the pavement. The two fence lines and the single pavement line were drawn to to reach the same vanishing, or horizon, point. If a second pavement line were drawn, it should touch the same point. Using two points, two pins, one on each side of the cartoon, you can draw two-point perspective. The horizon eye line is your position. For a top view, raise the eye line, and draw down from it. For a low horizon, looking up, place your eye line low, and draw the perspective lines down from it.

Try drawing a water glass. Hold it above your eye line, and you can see the bottom to draw it. With the glass even with your eyes, top and bottom circles seem like straight lines. Hold it low, and you can see the top.

F

Figure F: This "Adam 'n Evie" cartoon illustrates one-point-perspective drawing. Dotted line from Evie's eye to horizon point is used as a guide to determine the vanishing point, at which all horizontal lines converge, as shown here, and individual objects vanish.

You can approach caption writing in one of two ways. Write a funny line first, and then draw the characters in suitable poses. Or draw the characters in an interesting situation, and write the line afterwards.

The theme of "Adam 'n Evie" is that he is always doing the talking, explaining to her how the world really is. The fact that some of his explanations bear no relation to the truth is irrelevant—he has interpreted things to his own satisfaction, and this is all that matters to him.

Captions to illustrate

Try illustrating this line: "The world is like a big beach ball, Evie—only all the water is on the inside." Another: "I used to think dogs were boy animals and cats were girl animals. Now I'm not so sure." Or: "You bet it's a happy picture of me. Dad said if I didn't smile, he'd kill me."

"Guess what the Japanese have come up with now—FANS! No motors, no batteries, no nothing! You just hold them in your hand and wave them!"

Graphic Arts
Drawing a Comic Strip

The comic strips shown above were about a teenage character named Edgar Beever. First, the dialogue was written. Then balloons and lettering were drawn; after that, characters and backgrounds were drawn. Notice how the action, like camera angles, takes into consideration close-ups, long shots, angles of view, and even an amount of detail from panel to panel. The idea is to balance the strip. If the first drawing is a close shot with a simple background, the second panel can be farther away and have more detail. The third, for relief, has no background, and the fourth has plenty.

After the figures were roughed in with pencil, the hands, features, and details were inked in with black Indian ink and a fine-pointed flexible pen, which provides the greatest control. Clothing, objects, and backgrounds were inked in with a small sable brush. Lettering and balloon outlines were inked in with a narrow, flat-nib pen, heavy lettering with a wider pen.

If a mistake is made, wait for the ink to dry; then scratch off unwanted ink with a single-edge razor blade. Rub out carefully; then paint over the scratched-off area with Chinese white, using another small sable brush.

Always clean your brushes and pens when you have finished using them. If brushes dry with ink or paint on them, they become stiff and bristles break off. If pens are not kept clean, they clog.

In creating a comic strip, list your characters, exactly who they are and what their characteristics will be. This is not unlike writing a play. You should balance everything, even characters. Keeping their personalities consistent is difficult, but only at first.

Comic strips without words

Below are two examples of a comic strip without words. The action pictured in the panels carries the message. This is a particularly effective approach for children who cannot read. And it is comprehensible no matter what one's language. It is a throwback, in fact, to the early story drawings of the prehistoric artists.

The main ingredients in a comic strip without words, aside from the character or characters, are the location of the action and the props it provides. What the character does with the props is what conveys the story. Some of the best liked and most famous comic strips have been those that did not rely on words to get their meaning across.

I call the little character pictured here Tinker, because he loves to make things, to use objects in an imaginative way, and can always think his way out of impossible situations through a kind of improvised logic. It does not matter to him if his plotted fantasy does not work; the fantasy that develops instead is just as pleasing—or frightening.

The way to get ideas for cartoons is to become a people watcher or, in this case, a child watcher. Youngsters do some of the most wonderful and some of the silliest things imaginable. Always, however, their unfettered imaginations are working for them. They sit in an old tyre swing and they are in the basket of a huge balloon, drifting skywards. Tinker paints a pussycat with tiger stripes, below, and when it turns on him, it becomes a tiger. Washing off the stripes eliminates the threat.

Once you get the pattern, however, your own childhood imagination will flower again, and you can draw children even better. Real children are not always funny or ingenious. But the children in your imaginary world can be, because you make them so, and that is a great way of staying young.

These comic strips without words have only one character, Tinker. No words are needed to explain how he reacts to situations.

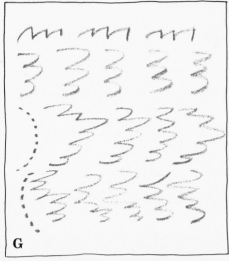

Figure G: Scribbled m's are the basis for impromptu cartoons. Do them vertically, linked continuously in curves, as shown by dotted lines.

Graphic Arts
Self-starter Cartoons

Blank paper is a threat all artists and writers must cope with. I have invented a way to eliminate it. The beginnings for cartoon faces in figure G were drawn by quickly scribbling m's sideways until they accidentally began to take on the features of cartoon characters. This is easy, although it does take a bit of practice. When you get the hang of it, you can scribble a couple of m's, and you are off and running. The phenomenon is that, once you have drawn the characters, your subconscious mind usually can supply funny lines for them to say.

In figure G, a series of script m's is written across the top. The second row shows the m's scribbled sideways like extended 3s. The next row shows the m's with added bumps, five or six this time, and extended to the right (note dotted line) to form something like a face. This would be the male face. The m's in the bottom row follow the convex dotted-line pattern, for the female face. The pointed bottoms of the m's provide sharper features.

In approximately the centre of a piece of paper, draw some extended m's as shown at left in figure H. Learn to make erratic bumps in the m's, so the features are somewhat different each time. The second sketch shows position of the eyes, which is very important—now the face takes shape. The next sketch (remember that a head is egg shaped) shows the finished heads, with hairstyles. Then, as in the fourth sketch, clothes and accessories are added.

Scribble . . .   **. . . add eyes . . .**   **. . . hair . . .**   **. . . clothes, and it's almost finished.**

Figure H: The apparently random scribbles at left, above, resolve into the finished cartoon below.

Figure I: Adding the background completes the drawing of the cartoon. All that remains is to think up a caption such as the one in the text, or you can reverse the process and think up your joke first.

Background details complete the picture (figure I). Now comes the magic: the funny line. Funny or not, you will have a good idea of what the man is saying. The reason? I believe your subconscious mind is funnier than your conscious mind. The line that came to me was: "I don't think my mother would believe I've taken up pipe smoking; she only lets me smoke cigars."

On the opposite page are three more cartoons developed from scribbled m's.

Cartoons as communication
One great value of cartoons is that they can communicate information in an amusing way. During World War II, for instance, cartoons instructed people in safety procedures and warned them against divulging secrets that might be useful to the enemy. The famous cartoon character known as Pilot Officer Prune was used by the Royal Air Force to teach fledgling pilots safe flying procedures. The lessons were both funny and unforgettable.

Once you have developed a cartoon technique, you will find many uses for it. You can make a cartoon collage to attract youngsters' attention and pound home some points. Any sign from "Brush Your Teeth" to "Put Out the Rubbish!" can become a friendly reminder rather than nagging if it is emphasized by a simple cartoon drawing.

"And you can tell your publisher I'm stopping the paper because I don't take to your editorial policies!"

"Oh, of course, I know your pipe drives the mosquitoes away, but I'm driving at fifty miles an hour!"

Cartoons in schools

Every teacher, I think, should have to pass a test in cartoon drawing. Bulletin boards with cartoons not only attract attention but make people feel better. Playful lampooning between teacher and student is healthy if done with cartoons. The school paper should always include some cartoons. Special announcements are less liable to be thrown away if they are enlivened by humorous or interesting drawings.

Cartoons in the office

Cartoons, with their striking quality, are a good way for management or staff to make points, and they help to keep morale high. Who is in the doghouse? A cartoon is the kindest way to tell. Who is king of the salesmen? A sketch of a man resembling the salesman and wearing a crown is a royal tribute. He will probably take it home and frame it.

Cartoons for community projects

Because cartoons tell their message so easily, they have long been used in advertising. Borrow from ad agencies' bag of tricks and use cartoons to make your point in community activities. Keep Our Town Clean committees in many communities have used cartoons to convey their message. P.T.A. meetings, grass-roots political campaigns, garage sales, and many other projects can be announced effectively by cartoons made by an interested amateur. Use an office duplicating machine to make copies for everyone.

Cartoons in decorating

Cartoon animals delight children and make good themes for children's rooms. They can be sketched small and enlarged for wall decorations by using the grid system described on page 127. Or sketch them from shadows projected by a magic lantern. Bold colour effects can be added with paint or patterned, self-adhesive plastic.

   You can use cartoons on furniture or screens, as wall hangings, as designs for needlework rugs or pillows. Draw them in ink, paint them, or make them in almost any medium, even painted glass with a crinkled-foil background.

"Then they called me in! 'Horace,' they said, 'if there's one man here who would know exactly what Tarzan would do in a case like this— it's YOU!' "

CARVING

Soap to Vegetables

by Jo-Anne Jarrin

Creative carving is the cutting away of material to produce a form or to decorate a surface. To a Michelangelo, this meant freeing a statue from the marble in which it was imprisoned. But lesser mortals working with more amenable materials must still have a feel for the material they plan to work with before they start to carve. Each substance has particular qualities of hardness, softness, and brittleness. Each has a different degree of responsiveness to cutting and shaping.

The easiest way for the beginner to learn about materials is to experiment with them. Explore them with your fingers and fingernails. Break off a portion of the material and examine the result. This will tell you how brittle the material is, and whether the break is irregular, or relatively clean and straight. Next, with a knife, find out how the material reacts to shallow and deep cutting, and to making intricate shapes which might crumble or collapse if the wrong material were used. As an example, the experienced soap carver knows better than to carve a figure with spindly legs that might collapse.

Soap and paraffin wax are good materials for the beginner to work with while he is learning basic carving techniques. They are relatively soft, and can be carved into three-dimensional shapes without encountering the problems of harder-to-work materials such as stone or wood. Soap and paraffin wax are more forgiving of mistakes, and permit repairs it would be difficult to make in harder materials. Their softness also permits experiment with rough, smooth, or textured finishes.

Another form of soft carving deals with the shaping of fresh fruits and vegetables, such as those shown in the projects beginning on page 34. Although they are far more perishable than objects carved of soap or paraffin wax, vegetables do provide the beginning carver with a variety of interesting substances with which to experiment. And, as so many carvers have found, much of the enjoyment of carving lies in the experimenting.

Carving and Moulding
Making Fish from Soap

Carving soap is not as easy as it might seem. As with any form of carving, the key to success is practice and a working knowledge of the medium. There are two main kinds of soap. One is the firm, Castile variety; the other, household soap, is softer and tends to crumble easily. Both varieties can be used successfully once you have become accustomed to working with them. Bear in mind that you will need a little practice and that any failures, as well as the chipped-away crumbs, can be saved and used for washing up.

Unwrap the soap, and let it stand about 24 hours in a dry place so excess moisture in the bar will evaporate. Do this with several cakes so alternatives will be available when you get down to work. A simple project to start with is the fish on page 32. Or sketch an original design on a sheet of paper. The simpler the design, the fewer the carving problems, especially for the beginner. Avoid too many angles or curves until you become more expert. Gather together a dull paring knife (a dull edge is easier to control), a felt marker, and a plate or tray to work on.

Punch-bowl pumpkin at top, pompon radishes and rosebuds, turnip pompon, celery stalk sections, carrot and cucumber pinwheels, spring onion brushes, tomato rose. (Directions on pages 34 to 37.)

1: Hold the knife with the blade almost parallel to the bar of soap. Trying not to cut deeply, shave off or shave out the brand name and any raised edges.

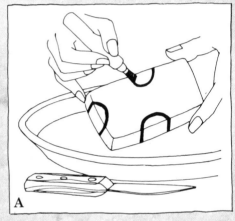

Figure A: Using a felt marker, draw three semi-circles on the soap. Continue the lines down the sides, as shown. Do not press with marker, or ink flow will stop.

Gently remove any markings from the soap, as shown in photograph 1. Then, if you are making the fish, mark the main cutting areas, as in figure A. When lines have been drawn, follow the directions with photographs 2, 3, 4, and 5 for carving. It is important that the main cuts, such as cutting away the semi-circles, be made evenly from front to back of the cake of soap. Never cut away a large area all at once. Unless you cut away gradually, you will risk breakage. Several shallow scoopings produce much less stress on the soap than a large gouge would. Also, shallow cuts are easier to control than deep ones. If a fairly large portion does break off, it can be re-attached by moistening along the break and holding the piece in place until dry. After you have shaped an area, smooth it with your fingers and a soft tissue.

2: Cut into the bar of soap until you have removed the entire semi-circle, from front to back. Work carefully, with gentle strokes, to prevent breakage.

3: To finish shaping the fish, carve head outlines, remove all sharp edges and round off corners. Make shallow, glancing strokes. Work the entire shape at once.

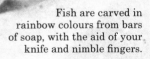

Fish are carved in rainbow colours from bars of soap, with the aid of your knife and nimble fingers.

4: Insert the knife point into one side of the head. Carefully twirl the knife to make a circular hole for the fish's eye. Repeat on the other side of the head.

5: Holding the head firmly, ease knife blade 1.5 cm into the soap. Just above this cut and angled down to meet it, make a second cut to complete the fish's mouth.

Carving and Moulding
Relief Design in Wax

Of the many waxes available, paraffin wax is the best for carving. You can buy it in small cakes or in large, economical slabs at art-supply shops. To carve a cake or slab in relief, as I did the fruit-bowl scene below, first trace your design on the wax with a toothpick. Then, using an angular gouge (figure B), cut along the lines that will be the deepest parts of the design. Next, use a curved gouge to shape the curved elements in the design, taking only small shavings with each cut until you have the shape you want. For small details, such as the grapes, try moving your hand closer to the tip of the gouge, as you would a pencil, for better control. Use a flat carving tool to shave away the larger background areas. Deepen the original cuts with an angular gouge if you find you do not have enough depth. Sweep away wax crumbs that accumulate as you work, with a soft bristle brush. Finish by gently rubbing highest areas with your fingers and a tissue. This will give the carving a translucent sheen.

To carve an object in the round from paraffin wax, melt wax in the top of a double boiler, pour into a cylindrical milk or soft drink carton, and place in cold water until wax hardens. Peel off carton, sketch object's outline on the block, as you did the fish, page 32, and you are ready to carve.

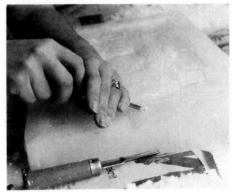

6: A good way to guide the tool is to place your free hand over its shaft as you move it slowly from behind. In this manner, you can maintain better control over the length and depth of cuts.

7: An alternative method is to place your free hand under the hand moving the tool. This will prevent overcutting. Never rest your free hand ahead of the tool; if you do you will risk a nasty cut.

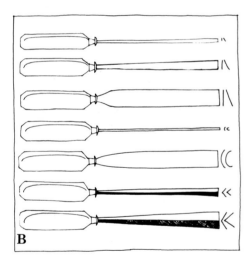

Figure B: A set of wax-carving tools. The top three are flat and are used to cut away large areas smoothly, as well as to produce well-defined outlines in the wax. Below these are two curved gouging tools, for scooping out curved portions. The last two are angular gouges, used to deepen outlines and details for better definition. A typical cut is shown at the right of each tool. It is not essential to have all of them, but at least one of each variety is recommended for successful wax carving. These sturdy and versatile tools can also be used to carve linoleum and wood blocks. They are not expensive and are available at art-supply and hobby shops.

8: The secret of making relief carvings such as this fruit bowl scene is to work slowly with small cuts or shavings, until you have obtained the shape you want.

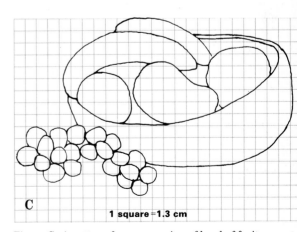

1 square = 1.3 cm

Figure C: A pattern for wax carving of bowl of fruit.

Foods
Carving Vegetables, Fruits

Carve the vegetables well in advance of your party or special meal, so you can give proper attention to shaping them. Placed in a bowl of ice water and stored in the refrigerator, they will keep for days.

Vegetable and fruit carving is said to have had its beginnings in the Far East, where the presentation of food played a significant role in its preparation and suitability for consumption. Because of religious beliefs concerning harmony and balance, food was supposed to appeal to all the senses, not only to the sense of taste. Following along these lines in the West, Antonin Careme, a master chef of the early 19th century, proposed the fundamental rule that the decoration should gracefully enhance and not overpower the dish. Decoration to stimulate the appetite can take a variety of forms, ranging from the artful placing of a sprig of fresh parsley to elaborate sculptural forms, from garnishing to creating delightful edible centrepieces. With a sharp knife, fresh fruits and vegetables, and some pre-party spare time, you can achieve impressive results.

Large, hard-skinned melons are ideal for carving and may be the focal point of a centrepiece. A watermelon can be formed into a serving bowl and filled

Skin is removed from rind of this pumpkin in a floral pattern to make a festive container for sweet cider or soup.

9: With a dark wax pencil, outline
your design on the pumpkin. Repeat the
motif around the circumference, making
sure to work within the boundary lines.

10: Use a curved gouge (see figure B,
page 33) to cut carefully along your
outlines (see also the photograph on page
30). Watch out for your fingers.

with scooped-out melon balls. A carved pumpkin can hold cold soup,
cider or pudding for an autumn lunch. It will not flavour the contents. The
only restriction is the seasonal availability of the fruit.

In working with a pumpkin, there are several considerations to note. If
you plan to fill it with food or drink, you must carefully remove the top
with a sharp knife and scoop out all except the firm outer flesh. (The seeds
may be kept and baked for an appetizing snack.) In this case, you cannot

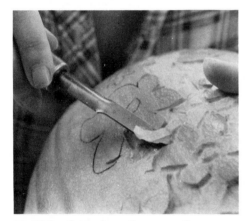

11: With a flat tool, gently remove the
skin outside each flower and in its centre.
No need to cut deeply: With the tool, simply
lift off the skin in these areas.

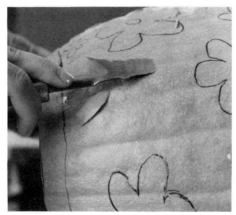

12: In large open areas between the
flowers, make long stroke with a flat
carving tool to remove big pieces of skin,
but keep clear of outlined areas.

keep the scooped-out pumpkin for more than three days, because it would
become soft and sag. If you wish to use the pumpkin repeatedly in
centrepieces, leave it intact. Several coats of varnish applied to the carved
pumpkin will enable you to keep it for an entire season.

When you are cutting the design into the pumpkin skin, use towels to soak
up the beads of moisture that will be released. If you wish, wear rubber
gloves to avoid getting this sticky substance on your hands. Draw boundary
lines around the circumference approximately 4 cm below the top and
above the base of the pumpkin. The floral patterns you cut should not extend
into these 4 cm spaces, so the pumpkin can be handled without damage
to the incised design. After you have carved the pumpkin, put it in the
refrigerator to keep it fresh until party time.

13: To make a turnip pompon, place peeled turnip between two wooden chopsticks on a cutting board. With sharp knife, slice thinly down to sticks, making parallel cuts.

14: Turn turnip, and cut across first slices at right angles, down to the sticks. When all cuts are made, place turnip in ice water. Petals of the pompon will open.

15: To make a radish rosebud, trim off the root tip. With the point of a sharp knife, cut petal shapes in the radish from the top to just above the base. Then slice down until each petal is freed.

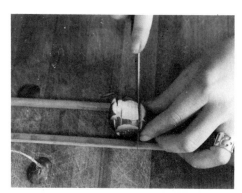

16: To make a radish pompon, place radish between two chopsticks, and cut crossed slices as you did the turnip. Then drop into ice water. Oblong radishes work best.

17: When you place a carved vegetable in water, check the temperature. If the water becomes warm, add several ice cubes. The water must always be ice-cold.

Carving small vegetables into floral forms, like those pictured in colour on page 30, requires a sharp knife and patience. A near-by bowl of ice water provides the magic to open vegetable flowers and crisp decorative accents such as carrot curls. Always prepare several more of each design than you will need, so that when you are arranging them in your centrepiece or as garnishes, you can select the best. The more you carve the more you will learn about the possibilities of particular fruits and vegetables. Working with turnips, for instance, might give you ideas about potatoes. The carvings described here are, for the most part, traditional floral forms.

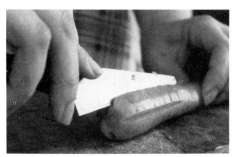

18: Clean and scrape a thick carrot. With a sharp knife, make V-shape lengthways grooves, evenly spaced, around the carrot. The grooves should be 3 mm deep.

19: When all grooves are cut, gently slice the carrot pinwheels. Each slice should be about 3 mm thick. Cucumber pinwheels are made the same way.

20: U-shape slices of celery are made with quick strokes of a knife held at an angle. Try to make slices wafer-thin.

21: Trim bulb and upper stalks from a spring onion. Make four cuts, 2.5 cm long, in each end. Immerse in ice water at once.

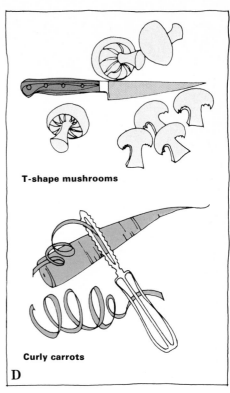

T-shape mushrooms

Curly carrots

D

But they should provide an inspiration for other designs. The Chinese, for example, carve the upper portions of extra-large carrots into miniature Buddhas. Before you know it, you will start looking at vegetables in the market with new eyes, alert to their carving and decorating potential.

The arrangement of your carved pieces is almost as important as the proper cutting. A primary rule is always to place your transformed vegetables and fruits on an undecorated dish or tray. Obviously, plates with coloured patterns would compete and divert attention from your work. If you do not have a solid-colour dish or tray, place a doily on a patterned one. A second rule is to avoid cluttering a dish. Several well-arranged plates will be far more attractive. If you want a more fanciful arrangement, try attaching your carved flowers with toothpicks, coloured with green food colouring, to whole vegetables, such as a head of lettuce or stalks of celery. Or combine your carved pieces with real flowers. Let your imagination run wild!

Figure D: Above, top, T-shape mushrooms are made by cutting thin slices from stem to cap. A drop of lemon juice stops discolouration. Above, coil carrot parings and pin with toothpick. Place in ice water. A gay garnish, they are nice in salads.

22: Tomato roses are made from ripe, firm tomatoes. Beginning at one end, peel off, trying not to cut too deeply into the pulp.

23: Shape tomato-skin strip into a rose. Pin with a toothpick. Place in ice water.

CASTING

Art of Repetition

by Toni and Dick Polich

The oldest known cast was probably made by a dinosaur. He stepped into clay, millions of years ago, and made a footprint. This cavity hardened and later was filled with fresh, liquid clay. When the liquid clay dried and solidified in the old cavity, it was a replica of the footprint. This prehistoric incident demonstrated three essentials of casting: the model (the foot), the mould (the old clay), and the cast (the new clay that solidified).

Later, man discovered that an object like a seashell, when pressed into clay, produced a cavity that had the negative shape of the seashell. Still later, he found that materials like hot wax and very hot metals would, as they cooled to a solid state, retain the shape of the cavity that contained them. It was not long before man applied these observations to duplicating solid objects that he treasured. He called this invention casting.

Man's earliest known casts were made with basically the same techniques that are employed today. A figure or object was modelled from a plastic material like clay or wax and allowed to harden. If clay, the hardened model was coated with some parting agent like tallow, then impressed into another chunk of fresh, moist clay. If wax, it was surrounded by liquid clay, with a drain-off channel left through the clay. In both cases, the clay moulds were allowed to dry and become solid. The embedded wax figure was removed by heating the clay and allowing the molten wax to run out of the channel provided, which explains why this method was called the lost-wax process. The cavities thus produced were negative duplicates of the original. The moulds were then filled with metal heated to the molten state. When the metal cooled and became solid, it retained the precise shape of the model.

The two casting projects that follow use the old techniques but substitute some new materials. In casting plaster, the mould used is of synthetic rubber and the cast is of plaster; both materials were unknown in their present form a hundred years ago. In casting metal, you will use plaster and tin, but still follow essentially the lost-wax process. Each method will duplicate your sculpture with great fidelity, preserving all the freedom and expressiveness you have given it. Both methods also produce casts that are far more durable than original sculptures made of modelling clay. The primary advantage of casting in plaster is that the mould is not destroyed in making the casting; hence several copies can be made from it. The primary advantage of using metal is, of course, that the casting will be even more durable than one made of plaster.

For each of the projects that follow, you will use a casting plaster sold under a variety of names, such as plaster of Paris, dental plaster, pottery plaster, and moulding plaster. Casting plaster hardens much more quickly than wall plaster, which should not be used for casting. If you plan to make several castings, you will find it more economical to buy 50 kilos of casting plaster from a large sculpture- or ceramics-supply outlet. Plaster can be obtained in the U.K. by mail order from Wengers Ltd, Etruria, Stoke-on-Trent, Staffs., or Alec Tiranti, 70 High Street, Theale, nr. Reading, Berks. But be warned that casting plaster does not keep well, so do not buy too much. You will need about 4.5 kilos for the plaster-casting project on pages 40 to 45, and 2.5 kilos for the metal belt buckle project on pages 46 to 49.

Liquid, flexible moulding compound is poured around a sculpted clay model inside the plaster container. As the compound hardens, it forms a mould for the final plaster cast.

Carving and Moulding
Casting a Head in Plaster

To make a cast about the size of the head shown at left, you will need 4.5 kilos or so of casting plaster, about 2.5 kilos of modelling clay (from an art-supply shop), and about 2.3 litres of polysulphide flexible moulding compound. Check the yellow pages of your telephone directory under the heading Plastics, Raw Materials, for companies that sell the moulding compound. One firm that sells it in the U.K. by mail is Smooth On Rubber (U.K.), Walter P. Notcutt, 44 Church Road, Teddington, Middlesex.

The moulding compound contains toxic substances. Do not put it in your mouth. Follow the manufacturer's instructions carefully and wear gloves for extra safety.

Other materials and equipment you will need are a plastic basin or bucket for mixing plaster; a disposable container for mixing the liquid moulding compound; a few pieces of cheesecloth or canvas to reinforce the plaster; a spatula to shape the plaster; a hammer and chisel to separate the plaster mould holder; a couple of old paintbrushes; a replaceable-blade modelling knife or scalpel to cut apart the flexible mould; some 4 cm wide flexible scrap-aluminium strips that can be cut into six 10 to 20 cm lengths and used as separators between the mould halves; four or five C-clamps, or 5 mm to 2.5 cm scrap metal that can be cut into 15 to 20 cm lengths and bent to form clamps, to hold the mould together; a plastic bag large enough to cover the model; about 225 g each of paraffin and petroleum jelly, which are used to keep materials from sticking together.

For finishing the cast, you will need a small tin of brown shoe polish and 250 ml of benzene for thinning it; a half kilo tin of paste wax; a small bottle of bronze powder; 500 ml of varnish.

Your first step in making the cast is to build a temporary plaster base for the clay model. The base should be a rough square, extending about 7.5 cm beyond the model on all sides. The volume of water you mix with 1 or 1.5 kilos of plaster to make the base should about equal the volume of plaster. Pour water into the mixing container first; then sift plaster through your fingers into the water. Continue sifting quickly until the plaster no longer sinks in the water, indicating that there is enough. Now let the mixture soak for two or three minutes, until the plaster islands become damp. Then stir briskly with your hands for a couple of minutes until no islands remain and the plaster has thickened slightly (photograph 1).

You have about 15 to 20 minutes to mix plaster and form the base before the plaster becomes too hard to use. So do not dawdle. When it has thickened slightly, put a glob of it on the work surface, and with the spatula roughly shape it into a square. If it runs, keep pushing it back until it starts to set. Add more plaster until the base is about 2.5 cm thick.

Sculpted head of modelling clay can be reproduced with all its subtle detail by making a casting of it in plaster.

Many sculptors like to work with modelling clay because it can be shaped easily. But it does not get very hard. So when work sculptured in modelling clay has been finished, it will frequently be cast in plaster to give it durability.

1: Mix casting plaster to make a temporary base for the model. If your skin is sensitive, it might be wise to wear rubber gloves or use a spatula while mixing.

2: Cover the model with a plastic bag to protect it from damage while the clay spacing layer and the plaster mould holder are being formed around the model.

Carefully set the clay model in the centre of the base while the plaster is still soft, so the model will sit solidly when the plaster dries.

Protecting the model
Give the model a coat of varnish to protect it; let dry. Using an old paintbrush, cover the model and the base with a coat of petroleum jelly, thinned half-and-half with paraffin. Heat this mixture in a double boiler until it is warm; then stir to make sure it is well blended. This coating will keep the materials to be added later from sticking to the model or its base. Cover the model (but not the base) with a plastic bag, as in photograph 2. This provides further protection against the temporary layer of modelling clay that you will fit around the model as the next step. This clay layer acts as a temporary spacer between the model and the plaster mould holder.

Next step is to roll out clay into slabs, 6 mm or less in thickness. Carefully fit the slabs around the model, as in photograph 3. Do not press hard against the model; you might damage it. The purpose is to establish a smooth wall covering the model, with an outer surface that has no cracks or corners that might interlock with the plaster you will apply later.

Next, build a small ridge around the vertical perimeter of the clay

3: Slabs of modelling clay form a wall around the model. The plaster mould holder is built over this wall. Then the plaster is split and the clay removed, leaving a space for the poured-rubber mould.

4: A thickened ridge is formed around the perimeter of the clay lining. Thin strips of aluminium inserted into this ridge make the parting line for the plaster mould holder. Strips are later discarded.

5: A new batch of casting plaster is mixed and applied to the clay liner to form the mould holder. Cheesecloth or canvas scraps are layered into the plaster to help to reinforce it.

covering the model, and form two clay horns at the top, as in photograph 4. These horns will provide the opening through which the flexible moulding compound will later be poured. Insert the thin 10 to 20 cm long aluminium strips into the centre of the clay ridge, working all the way around the ridge and letting the strips stick out 2.5 cm or more. These strips form a divider that will later enable you to pry the plaster mould holder apart.

Now coat the outside of the clay surface with the same mixture of paraffin and petroleum jelly that you used on the model and its base.

Making the mould holder
To make the plaster mould holder mix 2.5 kilos of plaster with water, following the procedure you used for mixing the plaster for the base. Apply a thin coat of wet plaster over the modelling clay. Reinforce wet plaster with a layer of canvas or cheesecloth; do not let cheesecloth cross the metal parting strips.

Apply another coat of plaster, more canvas, and more plaster, until the plaster is almost 2.5 cm thick, as shown in photograph 5. As you build up the plaster, form several flat areas on either side of the parting strips; these can be used later as clamping surfaces (see photograph 10, page 43).

Let the plaster mould holder air-dry overnight. When the plaster has hardened, it can be split into halves with a hammer and chisel; work chisel in along the edges of the metal parting strips, as in photograph 6. Remove these strips. If any modelling clay is stuck in the mould holder, remove it, as in photograph 7. Also, remove clay from the model. Set aside all this clay. Scour the mould holder's inner surface with steel wool. Fill any pinholes in the plaster (caused by air bubbles) with modelling clay, and smooth down. Then lubricate the inside of the mould holder (photograph 8) with the same mixture of petroleum jelly and paraffin used earlier. This will keep the liquid moulding compound from sticking to the mould holder. Drill two 1.5 mm holes for air vents near the bottom of the mould holder (see figure A).

When the mould holder is placed around the sculpted model, there is a cavity where the modelling clay had been (photograph 9). This cavity will be filled with the liquid compound that forms the actual mould you will later use for the casting. Clamp the two halves of the mould holder together around the model, and seal the cracks with modelling clay, as in photograph 10. For clamps, I used metal strips cut to 15 and 20 cm lengths, then bent into a U-shape and tapped over the opposing flat surfaces on the mould-holder sides. Large C-clamps would work as well. Or you could use clothes-line, belts, or even very heavy rubber bands to hold the two parts together. The important thing is that the parts are held together tightly and securely.

Now use modelling clay to secure short sections of cardboard tubing in the pouring holes left by the clay horns, as shown in photograph 10. These cardboard extensions will help to increase the pressure of the liquid moulding compound you will pour, forcing it more tightly around the mould.

Pouring the liquid moulding compound is the next step. You must mix enough to fill the cavity between the model and the mould holder in a single pour. You can judge the amount fairly accurately by the amount of modelling clay you used to create the original cavity and have set aside. Work this clay into the shape of the mixing container, and measure the depth. Then fill the container with moulding compound to this depth, plus 2 or 3 cm. Stir in the hardening agent according to manufacturer's instructions.

Pour the liquid moulding compound into the mould holder through one of

6: After plaster has hardened, mould holder is separated along metal parting strips. Work around the strips, using an old chisel or putty knife and light hammer taps.

7: When the mould holder is separated, remove the modelling clay from it and from the sculpted model. Smooth the inside of the holder with fine steel wool.

8: Lubricate the inside of the mould holder with petroleum jelly thinned with paraffin. This will keep poured flexible mould from sticking to the plaster.

9: Mould holder is placed around model, which also has been coated with thinned petroleum jelly to keep the flexible mould from sticking. Note space left by clay.

the cardboard tubes, as in photograph 11 and figure A. The other tube will let trapped air escape. Pour compound back and forth between mould holder and container to make sure crevices are filled. Then pour both tubes to the top. Let a little liquid trickle out of the drilled air-vent holes at the bottom, to show air has been forced out; then close vent holes with clay. Use a funnel, if necessary, to pour from a large container into the cardboard tube.

Set aside the mould holder for a day while the flexible moulding compound

10: The plaster mould holder is clamped around the model. Cracks are sealed with modelling clay. One cardboard tube lets trapped air escape; one is for pouring in liquid compound, which forms the mould.

11: Liquid compound is poured into the mould holder. Pour the compound back and forth between mould holder and container several times to fill all crevices. When the liquid hardens, it becomes the mould.

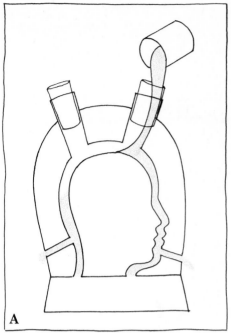

Figure A: Cardboard tube extensions, inserted in holes left in the plaster by the clay horns, allow more moulding compound to be poured in, increasing pressure to force compound around model.

12: After the plaster mould holder is removed, the flexible mould is sliced open to release the model. Cuts are made in centre of mould's thickened perimeter.

13: After the flexible mould is sliced apart, it is carefully pulled away from the sculpted model to avoid damaging it. The model is then removed.

14: Each half of the flexible mould is replaced in its matching plaster mould holder. Inspect the inside of the mould; remove any bits of clay that have stuck.

cures. When it has set, it will be dry but flexible, even rubbery. Open the mould holder again, cutting off the compound that penetrated the drilled air vents, to facilitate removal. Just leave the compound in the holes.

The most delicate operation of the project comes next: cutting the flexible mould apart to remove the model, as in photographs 12 and 13. With a very sharp tool—I used a surgeon's scalpel, but a modeller's replaceable-blade knife will do—slice into the centre of the thickened ridge. Work all the way around the ridge, and include the horns made by the pouring tubes. Cut carefully in a series of small slices, gradually increasing depth of slice. But be careful not to cut into the clay model inside. As you get nearly through the flexible mould, pull the rubber to stretch it away from the model as you slice. Once you have cut through in one place, it is easier to work

15: Mould holder, with flexible mould inside, is clamped and ready to receive the casting plaster. Here, U-shape metal bars clamp the mould holder together, but C-clamps or clothes-line would also work.

16: Fresh casting plaster is mixed for pouring into the mould. It is sifted into the water as described on page 40, then mixed to a creamlike consistency. Mould is turned bottom up for the pour.

17: Brace the mould holder with wood blocks, bricks or sandbags while plaster is poured in. Mix enough plaster to fill the mould. Start pouring immediately after mixing, before plaster can harden.

18: Pour the plaster back and forth between mould and container several times. This helps to fill all the crevices inside the mould and eliminate air pockets. Each time the mould is filled, shake it gently.

19: Remove the plaster casting when it has hardened. Unclamp the mould holder, and pull away the mould. Its flexibility will bend around undercut areas, which might lock with a more rigid mould.

your way around, stretching and cutting as you go. Make sure you have cut the rubber all the way around the perimeter of the mould, so that the two halves come apart like halves of a grapefruit. These halves form the actual mould. Remove the model and its plaster base. They are no longer needed for this project. Inspect the inside surface of the flexible mould carefully. Remove any particles of clay that may have come from the model. Be careful not to mar or tear any of the delicate ridges or crevices in the mould. These preserve the precise details of the original model.

Making the final casting
Place each flexible mould half back in its plaster mould holder, as in photograph 14, page 43. Be sure each is seated perfectly. Then fit the halves of the plaster mould holder together, and clamp them, as in photograph 15. Use the U-clamps or C-clamps as you did before, but this time you will not have to seal the side cracks with clay. The plaster will not work out through the tightly clamped seams of the flexible mould.

Turn the mould over, open end up, and brace it securely on the work surface. Now you are ready to make your first plaster casting. Follow the plaster-mixing procedure described on page 40, and mix 2.5 kilos of plaster to fill the mould cavity (photograph 16). It should be mixed to a consistency slightly thicker than heavy cream. Pour the plaster into the mould and then back and forth between the mixing bowl and the mould several times. You should also swirl it around in the mould, to make sure it gets into all the intricate nooks and crannies of the mould. Finally, fill the mould to the top (figure B). Brace the mould carefully so it will remain level and secure while the plaster hardens. Then leave the mould overnight or, better, a full day to allow the plaster to thoroughly cure and harden.

To extract the cast from the mould, remove the clamps, and pry open the mould holder as for the previous openings. Then remove the cast from the mould. It is not likely that there will be any mould marks; but if there are, scrape them away with a spatula or a fingernail. Inspect the cast carefully, and fill any air bubbles you find with wet plaster. Let the cast air-dry for a day or so while the surface hardens. If the cast feels even slightly damp or cool against your face, it is not dry.

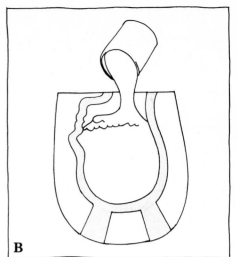

Figure B: With mould turned upside down and well braced, plaster is poured into bottom opening, then poured back and forth several times between mould and container to make sure it gets into all the crannies of the mould.

20: The plaster cast is finished by varnishing, rubbing with shoe polish to bring out relief, adding bronze powder for highlights, coating with paste wax and buffing lightly.

Finishing the cast

The final step, when the cast is completely dry, is to finish it. Here, you can pretty much let your imagination be your guide. The cast can be simply sealed with varnish if you wish. Or it can be spray painted with car spray finish, antiqued, waxed, or even stained. My choice was to seal the plaster with varnish and then apply rubbed-on brown shoe polish, thinned with a little benzene, as in photograph 20. The finish was then rubbed gently to bring out the relief; too much rubbing dulls the edges of the cast. Bronze powder was then dusted on and gently rubbed to produce attractive highlights. Finally, a coat of paste wax, warmed in a double boiler to make it thinner, was applied and buffed slightly with a soft cloth. The final effect achieved is that of a warm, glowing, metallic patina.

Mounting the cast

Although the bust in this project did not necessarily call for mounting on a base, that can easily be done. Leave the mounting surface free of finish, and apply two-part epoxy glue. Then glue it to a wood or marble base, cut to a size appropriate for your sculpture. The base should not be so large or bulky that it dominates the sculpture, which is, after all, what you want people to notice first. You can probably cut and finish a wood base yourself. If you want marble, a local supplier of headstones can cut one for you.

Carving and Moulding
Casting a Belt Buckle

A metal belt buckle cast by the lost-wax process can be as simple or as elaborate as you wish. To make it, you will need about 2.5 kilos of casting plaster, half of a 4 by 24 by 30 cm block of sculptor's or modelling wax, obtainable from Alec Tiranti (see page 38), and 2.5 kilos of tin (look under Tinplate or Scrap Metal Merchants in the yellow pages of your telephone directory). Tin can be melted on a kitchen stove, retains details crisply, and, when used for a belt buckle, looks much like silver.

Sketch the outlines of the belt buckle and your design to fit within those outlines. Figure C shows my version. Then cut off a piece of sculptor's wax, and warm it between your hands. Pat the warmed wax into a slab 3 mm to 1 cm thick and large enough for you to cut the length and width of the buckle from it. With a sharp knife, cut the outlines of the buckle from the slab. Then, with the knife or a sharp pencil, incise in the front of the wax buckle any background designs you wish to add. If you would like to imprint background textures on any areas of the design (using a wire screen, for example), this is the time to do it. Bend the slab so its outside is slightly convex, to fit the curvature of the waistline.

Add the relief components of the design to the front of the buckle by sticking small bits of wax on the buckle slab. In the case of the flower design shown, the centre and each petal were separate pieces of wax, pressed into place and shaped. Even though some of these protrude and are curved, they will be reproduced faithfully in the metal. For the belt loop, roll a small piece of wax into a cylinder about 3 to 6 mm in diameter. This can be attached to one end of the buckle, as shown below, or fixed at right angles to the back of the buckle. In the latter case, the tail end of the belt will come through the loop again and end on the outside. In the former case, the tail end will be under the belt and fastened with a pin fitting through a hole in the belt.

If you place the belt loop on the end of the buckle as I did, the necessary small pin in the end opposite the loop, on the back, cannot be moulded as part of the buckle, because plain tin is not strong enough. Make the buckle slab slightly thicker where the pin will mount (see figure D) to provide

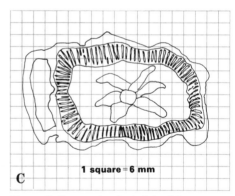

Figure C: Pattern for the belt buckle shown in the colour photograph.

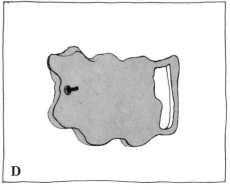

Figure D: Rear side of the buckle, showing the location of the pin that fastens into a hole in the belt.

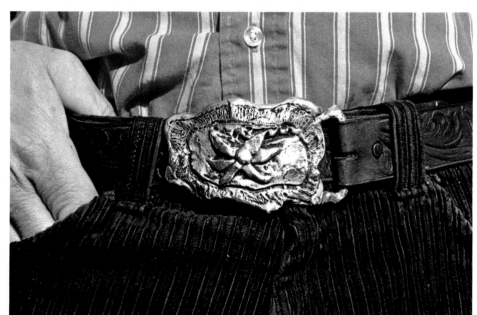

This belt buckle was originally created in sculptor's wax and then cast in solid tin by the lost-wax method. The work was done in an ordinary kitchen.

reinforcing for mounting a steel pin in the buckle (one of the last steps). You thicken the area where the pin will mount by pressing a piece of wax, half the size of a pea, on to the back of the buckle slab. Smooth its edges into the wax of the buckle body, but do not press it too flat.

When the buckle modelled in wax is completed, it is necessary to build with wax the passageways that will let the molten metal reach the buckle and also let trapped air escape. The larger passageways are called runners, and the smaller ones are called air vents. At the top of the main vertical runner, a waxed paper cup is attached to create an enlarged pouring hole, called a sprue. The runners, air vents, and sprue are assembled into the treelike structure shown in figure E. Remember that everything you make of wax will be a cavity in the final mould. The purpose is to permit the molten metal to flow easily into all parts of the mould and to let the air and gases escape so they will not make voids or bubbles in the casting.

The runners and air vents can be formed out of warm wax, or buy wax rods and sticks from a craft-supply shop and cut them to appropriate lengths. Make the main runner and the two short ones from a wax stick 1.5 to 2 cm in diameter. The short runners will support the wax buckle. Attach side runners at right angles to the main runner, as in figure E.

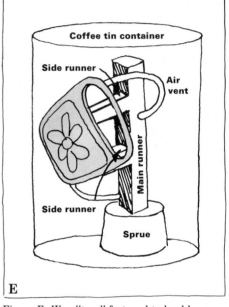

Figure E: Wax "tree" fastened to buckle model. This is how the wax buckle and its supports are placed in a container before the plaster that forms the mould is cast.

21: Make the body of the wax buckle by softening wax in palms, shaping into a slab, and cutting out. Then incise background designs on buckle surface.

22: Add flower design by making the centre and each petal separately, then pressing into place while soft. Then form belt loop, and attach it to one end.

23: Container placed around the wax structure will hold the casting plaster that forms the mould. Both container ends are open. The container's bottom is sealed to a board with modelling clay so the plaster you pour will not work its way out.

24: Mix casting plaster to a creamy consistency, and pour into the container around the wax model and over it, making sure to fill every nook and cranny. Fill the container to the top. Let mould dry out for several days before proceeding.

25: Place the dry plaster mould in an 80°C oven for several hours to melt out the wax model inside it. Use a drip pan below it to catch melting wax. Empty the pan at frequent intervals.

26: Tin can be melted in a cast-iron pot on top of the stove. Stir and melt in 1 metre of 12-gauge copper wire to give the tin added strength. The process of melting the tin takes about half an hour.

The wax model of the buckle and its wax supports are perfectly reproduced in hard metal. This is a simple design, but quite intricate castings can be made by the lost-wax method.

The technique of attaching or welding wax pieces to each other is applying a hot knife to joining areas, then pressing them together. Weld the inside of the buckle slab to the ends of the short runners, as shown in figure E, page 47. Now roll out two 3 mm diameter wax rods. Attach one to a top corner of the buckle and the other to a bottom corner of the buckle, and bend them so they can be attached to the main runner (see figure E). These are the passageways that help to prevent air and molten wax from being trapped inside the buckle mould.

For the pouring hole or sprue, place a small waxed paper cup, upside down, on a wax coated card or piece of metal. Seal the bottom of the wax stick that is the main runner to the bottom of the cup, as in figure E.

The treelike wax structure must now be encased in plaster to make the mould. You will need to place a container around the wax structure to hold the plaster you will pour. Use a kilo coffee tin with both ends removed for a container. Put the wax structure on a piece of wood, and place the container over it. Seal the base of the container to the wood with modelling clay.

Now mix 2.5 kilos of casting plaster according to the instructions on page 40. Pour it around the wax structure, using a brisk and continuous motion so every crevice and corner of the wax model will be filled. Let the plaster air-dry for at least three or four days. When dry, it will not feel cold or damp against your skin.

To melt the wax out of the plaster mould, place the mould, opening down,

27: Pour the molten metal into the mould, which was already pre-heated to melt out wax. Use a steady pouring motion. Place the mould on scrap plywood to minimize any damage if the metal spatters.

28: After pouring the molten metal, let it cool for an hour. Then place the mould in a bucket of cold water. Water softens the plaster, which you then chip away from the casting with hammer and chisel.

in a shallow container, and place both in the kitchen oven. Heat oven to about 80°C, but no higher. Check frequently, and as melted wax accumulates in the pan, empty it. At this temperature, there is little danger, but there could be unpleasant smells if wax accumulated. When no more wax comes out, turn the mould on its side, and let it heat another hour. Then turn it upside down again, and heat for another hour, to remove trapped pockets of wax. Turn it on the other side, and heat again for an hour. When no more wax can be coaxed out, turn the mould upside down again, and turn the oven up to 200°C, to burn out residual wax that has soaked into the plaster. Heat for about an hour.

As the mould heating is going on, prepare for the metal pouring. Place chunks of tin in a cast iron pot, and place pot on a stove burner at high heat. It will take about half an hour to bring the metal to melting point.

In handling molten tin or lead, wear asbestos gloves or use enough pot holders to insulate against the heat for at least two minutes. Some metal might splatter in pouring, so it is wise to wear protective safety glasses, high-top leather shoes, and long trousers tied around the ankles.

When the metal is molten, remove the plaster mould from the oven, and

29: With a hacksaw, cut off the excess metal left by the vents and pouring gates. Hold work securely in a vice, and cut as close as possible to the buckle. Save the excess metal for future castings.

30: File away remaining excess metal from the buckle back. Finish the cuts with fine aluminium-oxide abrasive paper. To make hooking pin, drill a pilot hole for a small screw; insert it, and cut off head.

31: Finish the metal casting of the buckle by rubbing with fine steel wool, then rubbing with an emery cloth. To bring out the relief of the design, rub black shoe polish into the crevices, and wipe away the excess.

place it on a 60 cm square piece of plywood, on the floor. Seat the mould securely with the cup opening (sprue) facing up. Poise the melting pot's pouring spout or lip over the opening, and pour in one continuous motion until the mould is full to the top of the cup hole with molten metal.

Let the mould stand for an hour before trying to remove the casting. The metal will solidify in minutes, but will remain dangerously hot much longer. After an hour, pick up the mould with potholders, and place it in a bucket of cold water. This will both cool the metal and soften the plaster mould. Remove the coffee tin container, and with hammer and chisel, carefully chip away the plaster. Work from the sprue downwards and take care not to damage the metal parts. Use a long thin screwdriver or metal knitting needle to remove any plaster in crevices.

Next, install the retaining pin in the buckle (figure D, page 46). Drill a 3 mm hole about half way through the buckle, from the inside. The pin is a No. 6 by 2.5 cm steel screw. Cut off the threaded point so the length of the remaining threads equals the depth of the hole. With a screwdriver, turn the screw into the hole. It will cut its own threads in the soft metal. Use a hacksaw to cut off screw's shank 1 cm from the buckle. File cut end smooth.

Polish the buckle with fine-grade steel wool. Then rub black shoe polish into the background details to bring out the design. Wipe off excess, and polish again. Spray with water-clear varnish to preserve the lustre.

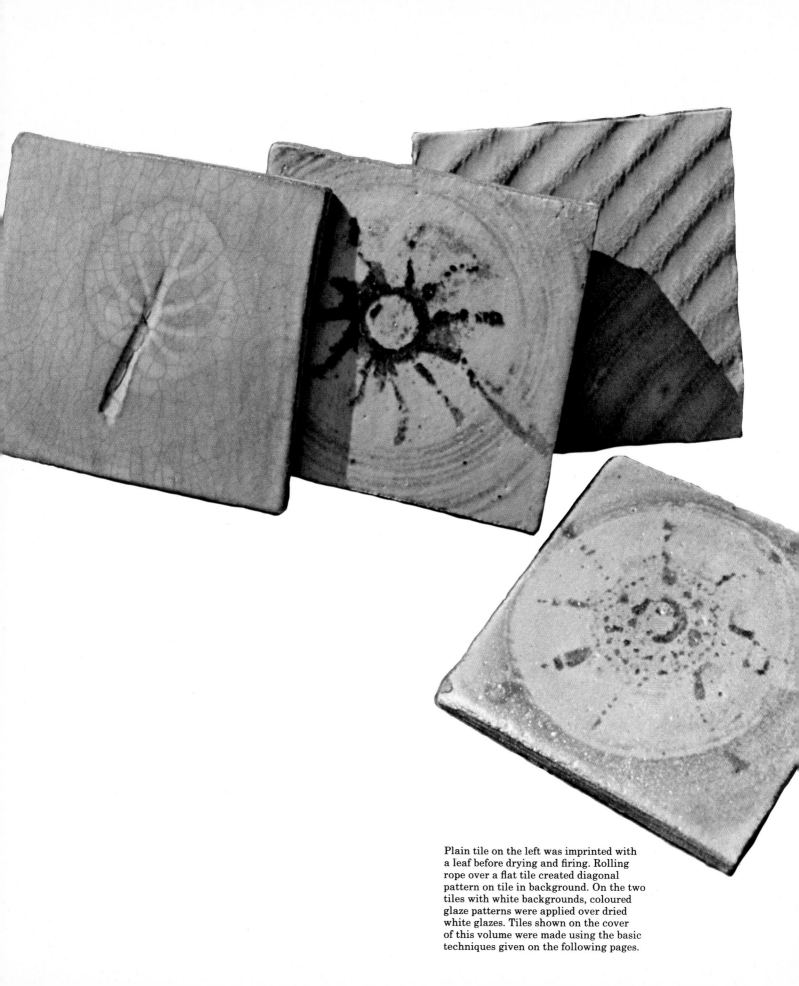

Plain tile on the left was imprinted with a leaf before drying and firing. Rolling rope over a flat tile created diagonal pattern on tile in background. On the two tiles with white backgrounds, coloured glaze patterns were applied over dried white glazes. Tiles shown on the cover of this volume were made using the basic techniques given on the following pages.

CERAMICS

Commencing with Clay

by Martha Longenecker

Working with clay is one of man's oldest crafts. Even before recorded history, man had discovered how easy it is to shape useful and beautiful objects from this material that is plastic when it is moist. When it has dried, it becomes hard enough to hold its shape indefinitely. Firing it in a kiln gives it a stonelike durability that can last for centuries, as the many tile and pottery pieces left by ancient civilizations attest.

The resistance of fired clay (ceramics) to water, salt, acids, heat, and cold also makes it an ideal material for containing food and drink. But it is the ease with which clay can be formed into varied shapes—and decorated with myriad colours of glazes—that attracts the craftsman. Even beginners can enjoy making the colourful tiles, bowls, and openwork coat hooks shown on the opposite and following pages.

While the primitive potter had to make do with the clay he found along the river bed, today's home ceramist has a variety of pre-mixed clays available. These divide into three basic types. The first clays are those used to make earthenware; they can be fired at 1000 to 1200°C to help to bond them, but they will still remain porous. The second clays are those used to make stoneware; these can be fired at a higher temperature (1200 to 1300°C), so that they vitrify and lose porosity. The third clays are used to make porcelain; these can be fired at 1280 to 1460°C to produce the translucency typical of fine china.

The porcelain clays are less pliable and harder to work with, and they are more liable to crack when fired. Both the earthenware and stoneware clays are easy to work. Of the two, the stoneware clays are less porous and more durable. So, for the projects that follow, I recommend stoneware clays.

You can make all the projects in this entry from 12 kilos of clay. Ceramic-supply shops and studios, and some hobby shops and department stores, stock this size. Make sure the block you buy has been kept sealed and moist in an airtight plastic wrapper. Check the label; if this indicates a firing range between "cone 6 to 10" (see page 54), the clay is for stoneware.

Clay also comes in many colours, an important factor if you plan to leave a piece uncoloured by glaze. Ask at the shop to see sample chips showing the various colours of clay before and after firing.

Ceramics
Making Clay Tiles

The tiles shown in the colour photograph opposite were cut from rolled-out slabs of clay. To cut out 15 tiles similar to those shown, you need, in addition to the clay, two 56 cm lengths of 2.5 by 1.3 cm wood strips to form the edges of the clay slab from which the tiles are cut. You also need a 40 cm length of 2.5 cm dowel, or a wooden kitchen rolling pin, which is used to roll out the slab; a long ruler; a plastic triangle; and a dull kitchen knife.

The first step in making the tiles is preparing the clay. You should add a ground-up fired clay, called grog, to the fresh clay. The grog makes the clay more porous, helping any air bubbles in the clay escape. In rolling out slabs, inexperienced ceramists frequently leave small air bubbles in the clay. These bubbles may later explode during firing, ruining the project. You can purchase clay with grog already mixed into it, or mix your own. Grog

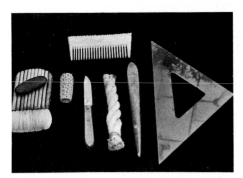

1: Some suggested equipment to use in beginning to explore ceramics includes wide, soft brush, smooth stone (resting on brush), ceramic bead with raised pattern for imprinting, vegetable knife, comb, segment of rope, pointed clay-modelling tool, and plastic triangle. Ceramic-supply shops carry modelling tools and ceramic beads or other objects to be used for imprinting. (Other equipment will be noted as it is needed for particular projects.)

is available from the same ceramic-supply shops that stock clay, and 12 kilos of grog is ample for kneading into 11 kilos of clay. But take the time to make sure the grog and fresh clay are well blended.

The clay mixture for the tiles should not be so stiff that it cracks when you bend a piece of it. It should not have any lumps or hard pieces. It should not be sticky, but just soft enough so you can mould and form it with your fingers. Working on oilcloth that has the face side down, knead the clay, until it is the right consistency. If it is too hard and dry, add water, and work it into the mix.

When the mix is the right consistency, you are ready to make the slab for the tiles. Position the two 2.5 by 1.3 cm wood strips parallel to each other and 30 cm apart, with the 1.3 cm dimensions facing, and nail together. If you have laid your oilcloth on a good table, put a piece of scrap wood under the cloth to protect the table surface. Next, pinch off a handful of the clay mix, as in photograph 2, and push it down against the oilcloth between the two wood strips. Press the clay down hard with the heel of your hand, as in photograph 3, to eliminate any trapped air. Continue adding handfuls of clay, pressing them down and smoothing them until you have filled the space between the wood strips and have formed a rough clay slab. The slab should be about 54 or 56 cm long and 2 cm high, slightly above the wood strips.

Now place the length of dowel across the two wood strips, and begin rolling it back and forth over the clay to even the surface, as in photograph 4. Rolling will be somewhat difficult at first, but it becomes easier as the clay levels out. If the clay begins to accumulate on the dowel, scrape it off before doing any more rolling. Make sure underneath surface is also smooth.

When your slab has been rolled to a uniform thickness and is smooth on both sides, run the knife along the edges, between the clay and the wood

2: When the clay mixture is the right consistency (see text), pinch off a handful, and press it down on a work surface covered with face-down oilcloth.

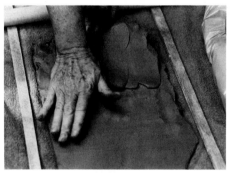

3: Press clay down between two side strips, using heel of hand to force out trapped air. Continue adding clay until area between the wood strips is filled.

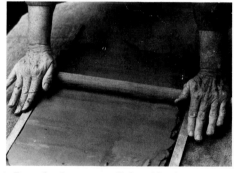

4: Press firmly as you roll dowel back and forth until the slab has a uniform thickness and smooth surface. Scrape clay pieces off dowel if they accumulate.

5: After squaring off end of slab, using a plastic triangle and ruler or wood side strip, cut through clay with a knife, as shown. Use side strip as guide.

6: Remove side strips, and with triangle and ruler, divide slab into 15 10-cm squares. Cut out tile squares, using the triangle or ruler for a cutting guide.

7: Gather clay scraps left from trimming slab; press into a ball; put in a plastic bag, and seal the bag. If clay has dried, moisten it before sealing the bag.

Ceramic tiles do not have to have flat surfaces. They can be textured in a variety of interesting ways, as these tiles suggest.

strips, to free the strips from the clay. Next, square off one end of the slab. Use the plastic triangle and the ruler or one of the side strips to make sure the line you mark is at right angles to the sides of the slab. Working close to the end of the slab, mark the end line lightly with the tip of the knife blade. Then, using the ruler or wood strip as a firmly held guide, cut through the clay with the knife as in photograph 5. Next, measure and mark 51 cm from the end of the slab you have just cut. Use the knife point to lightly incise a line that runs through this mark at right angles to the sides of the slab. This line marks the other end of the slab. Cut it as you did the first end.

With the sides and ends of the 30 by 51 cm slab established, divide the slab into 10 cm squares. Use the ruler and triangle, as you did for the slab ends, to make sure that horizontal and vertical lines are at right angles to each other. Next, using the ruler or triangle as a guide, cut through the clay along these lines with the paring knife, as in photograph 6.

Before decorating the tiles, gather the scraps of clay left from cutting out the tiles (photograph 7); slap them together to keep air from being trapped within, and press them into a ball. Place the ball in a sealed plastic bag for later use. If the clay has become too hard to work easily, poke holes in it, and knead in some water before sealing the clay in the bag.

As an alternative to the flat slab and the flat tiles it produces, you might try a variation like that shown in photograph 8. Or try rolling a short section of stout rope over a flat tile (see colour photograph, page 50). Other texture variations are shown in the photograph above. You can also trace and cut different shapes of tiles (see the cover of this volume).

8: Instead of using a smooth surface, roll out the clay slab on a woven mat to achieve interesting texture on the front or back. You can roll out clay on any woven fabric, macramé, or non-stick material that has an unusual texture.

9: To decorate tile before firing, brush slip, made by thinning a contrasting coloured clay with water, over wet tile. Cut through slip to make what is termed as graffito design (photograph 10).

10: Use an orange stick to make lines; cut through the light-coloured slip so dark clay shows through and forms an interesting geometric pattern that can be repeated on other tiles (photograph 11).

11: Scratch identical designs on four tiles. Place together, sides touching. Use stick to re-define the lines; then roll the surfaces with a piece of dowelling to soften the pattern. Next, the tiles are air-dried, then bisque fired.

After you have formed the tiles, they must be air-dried before being fired. This is true of all clay projects, however they are made. Flat pieces such as tiles should be placed on newspaper or some other absorbent material to dry, and turned occasionally to prevent warpage. As the moisture evaporates from the clay, the tiles shrink, usually between 10 and 15 per cent. Keep this in mind if relatively accurate dimensions are needed for the finished product. (For example, to make sure your 15 tiles would be quite close to 20 cm square after they had dried, you would have had to use a 34.3 by 57.3 cm slab of clay and divided it equally into 15 squares. But such precision is not usually required.) Once the tiles are totally dry, they are ready to be fired.

There are some methods of decorating tiles that you can use before firing, indeed even before the tiles are dry. One is to brush a thin coat of a contrasting colour of liquid clay, called slip, over the still-wet tiles, as in photograph 9. Then use an orange stick from a manicure set to cut a design through the slip, so the colour of the original tile shows through, as in photographs 10 and 11. You can mix your own slip by simply thinning clay with water until it has a creamy consistency. (In contrast, the slip used for joining the clay pieces on pages 57 to 61 is thick and pastelike.)

Firing the clay

Firing ceramics serves two purposes: It permanently bonds the clay, and it melts and fuses glazes on to clay surfaces. But the two processes are usually achieved in separate steps involving two firings. The first firing, which takes about eight to ten hours, is called the bisque or biscuit firing; the second, which takes six to ten hours, is called the gloss or glaze firing. If glaze will not be used, the clay can be decorated with slip when wet, then air-dried and fired only once (bisque fired). It is also possible to glaze a clay piece before it is bisque fired; but the two-step firing is more generally used when glazes are involved, because it allows better control of the clay and the glaze colours.

Firing is done in a kiln, which is an oven furnace used for ceramic work of all types. While home kilns may be purchased from ceramic-supply outlets, they are expensive (£100 and up), and the techniques of firing are complex. Kilns must be loaded in a special way, and the firing times and temperatures vary with the type of ware and the kind of firing, either bisque or glaze. For these reasons, the amateur ceramist is better off using the firing services provided by commercial studios and ceramics-supply outlets. These places charge a modest fee based on the size and number of pieces and the temperature at which they are to be fired. You can keep the cost down by having stoneware pieces fired at lower earthenware temperatures; but the fired pieces will then be more porous than if they had been fired at the higher stoneware temperatures.

Ceramic pieces should never be fired at a higher temperature than the upper limit specified for the type of clay used. For earthenware, this would be 1200°C; for stoneware, 1300°C. If fired above these temperature limits, the clay piece will melt and deform.

To monitor temperatures achieved in firing, pyrometric cones are placed in the kiln. These are so made that they bend at specific temperatures, signalling that the temperature inside the kiln has reached that temperature. The cone designations you will see on the labels of many pre-packaged clays indicate the firing ranges for that clay. Thus, Seger cone 6 to 10 indicates that the clay is stoneware to be fired at 1200 to 1300°C. Cones 05 to 6 indicate earthenware; cones 9 to 16—1280 to 1460°C—indicate porcelain.

Glazing

After pieces have been bisque fired, they are ready for glazing. Glaze is a glass-like coating that is melted and fused to the surface of clay. Glazes are made from inorganic substances like lead, soda, borax, and feldspar, mixed

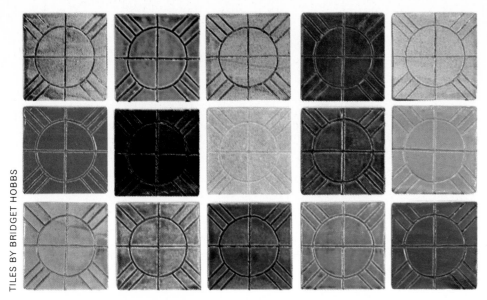

TILES BY BRIDGET HOBBS

This range of tiles shows some of the colours which may be obtained from four main colouring oxides, in various base glazes. They are cobalt (blue shades), copper (greens) and iron and manganese (shades of brown and yellow).

with metallic oxides for colour. An almost infinite variety of colours and effects can be achieved with glazes. The range of colours is made by the combination of different metal oxides. Most oxides are toxic when taken by mouth, but glazes should be quite safe after firing at stoneware temperatures or higher. Do not put glazes into your mouth, and wash carefully after using them. In addition to the different oxides used, glaze is affected by many other variables, including the type of clay used and the kiln temperature.

Glaze can be mixed to a creamy consistency for brushing over clay, or thinned with water for dipping, spraying, or pouring over clay surfaces. As a general guideline, for tile decoration the glaze should be brushed on until it is about a millimetre thick.

The white-and-blue tiles pictured on page 50 illustrate one popular method of applying glaze to achieve a special effect. A coat of white glaze is first brushed over the bisque-fired tiles. When the glaze has dried enough to lose its sheen, the additional colours (in this case, blue and yellow) are brushed on in the design desired. The tiles are then glaze fired.

Another popular technique for glazing bisque-fired tiles is called the wax-resist method. First, a design is painted on the tile, as in photograph 12, with a liquid wax you can obtain from a ceramic-supply shop. The waxed areas will not absorb glaze applied over them, hence the name wax-resist. Next, a thin layer of prepared cobalt-and-iron glaze is brushed over the whole tile, as in photograph 13. The glaze is allowed to dry and is then fired. The waxed pattern will show through quite clearly in the finished piece after firing.

In applying glaze, make sure that none gets on the back of the tiles; if it does, wipe off with a damp sponge, or the tiles will stick to the kiln shelves during the firing period.

Sources for glaze
The amateur ceramist would do well to consult a ceramic studio or a ceramic-supply shop on the types of glaze needed to achieve certain effects and how the glazes should be applied. These sources can also supply the glazes, which usually come in powdered form. They can be mixed with water and applied at home. Once you have applied a glaze, the sources may be able to do the glaze firing for you for a fee.

12: To decorate tiles with the wax-resist method, with a soft brush paint a design in liquid wax (from ceramic-supply shop) on a bisque-fired tile. Waxed areas will not absorb glaze applied over them. Let wax dry a few minutes before glazing.

13: After painting design on tile with liquid wax, brush a thin layer of prepared cobalt-and-iron glaze over the entire tile. Notice how flower design shows through the glaze. Let glaze dry a few minutes. Then have glazed tile fired.

Ceramics
Making a Clay Bowl

A shallow clay bowl can be made by adding another technique to those already learned in making simple tiles. After you have rolled out an even clay slab, using the strip-and-dowel method (photographs 2 to 4, page 52) cut out 20 by 30 cm oval freehand. Imprint a design on it; then place it on a plastic-covered pillow, and adjust it to the desired curvature. You can also use a sling, basket, or sand to support the clay. Do not remove the bowl until the clay holds its shape (becomes leather-hard). This usually takes several days, longer if the weather is damp or cool.

Use a dull table knife to trim or scrape the edges and remove any rough spots. Burnish (shine) the surface with a smooth stone. Cut a handle as in figure A. Let dry thoroughly, then bisque fire at a stoneware temperature. Brush matt-white glaze over the inside; then remove excess with paper towelling, leaving glaze only in the grooves if you have chosen to add them. Proceed with glaze firing. The bowl can be used in an oven, as a serving dish, or as a wall decoration by hanging it from a wire run through the handle.

14: Draw freehand and cut an oval, about 20 by 30 cm, from a clay slab 1.3 cm thick. With a wide hair comb, swirl texture through the centre of the form. The bowl can be made any size you wish.

15: Place the imprinted clay oval in a depression in a plastic-covered pillow. Arrange pillow until the curvature of the bowl pleases you. Do not remove the bowl until clay reaches a leather-hard stage.

16: To polish or burnish the bowl, first dampen the surface. Then rub with a smooth stone to push all small particles below the surface, leaving a satiny finish. Bowl can now be bisque fired.

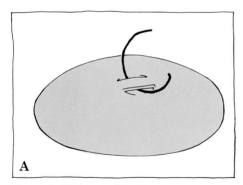

A

Figure A: With a small knife, cut two shallow half-circle indentations in back of bowl. Use wire to remove clay between lower portions of half circles, leaving a bridge that forms a handle, as shown.

It is only one more step from making a tile to making a decorative, useful bowl.

Ceramics
Making a Coiled Bowl

by Paula Johansson
Making containers with coils of clay is an ancient method used by artisans long before the invention of the potter's wheel. Ceramic pieces that leave many spaces, like the bowl made with coils, are called openwork: the product is lighter and more delicate than solid-clay work. Everything except the firing can be done in your kitchen, garage, or back garden.

Stoneware clay is recommended for both coil projects—the bowl and the

This ceramic bowl is made of interlocking repetitions of a simple flower shape.
Elements are cemented together with a thin mixture of clay and water, called slip.

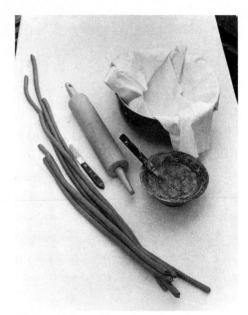

17: Materials used in openwork projects: rolled clay coils; knife for cutting; rolling pin; kitchen fork for scoring pieces to be slipped together, shown here in a bowl of slip; and large bowl and fabric, within which clay bowl is formed. You will also need a container in which to mix the glazes.

coat hooks on pages 60 and 61. Work with clay hard enough to keep its shape but soft enough to be rolled easily into long coils. Roll several 60 cm long coils by hand. Curl them to form five-petalled flowers, each 12 cm in diameter. As you form a flower, press centre as in photograph 19. This pushes the centre firmly together and flattens it slightly, making the flower uniform in depth. In a kitchen bowl about 30 cm in diameter and 15 to 20 cm deep, put a piece of fabric. Place one flower shape in the bottom of the bowl; add the others one at a time. Joining pieces before they are fired requires thick slip, clay mixed with water to a paste-like consistency. Although there are tools designed for slipping (joining), I prefer an old table fork. Use the tines to scratch or roughen surfaces that will touch. Dab slip on these areas, and push the pieces firmly together. Remove excess slip with your finger or the fork. Parts of any assembled clay project must always be well slipped together to keep them from separating during firing. Continue slipping flower shapes together in the bowl until the inside is covered. Let dry until the clay is leather-hard. With the fabric, lift clay bowl out of the kitchen bowl. Make a base by bending a coil to make a double circle 12 cm in diameter. Roll several clay balls, and flatten them on the outside of the coils for decoration. Slip the bowl on to the base. Let dry for several days. Have the bowl bisque fired at a stoneware temperature.

In separate containers, mix prepared powdered glazes with water to a creamy consistency. Dip the bowl into matt-white glaze, keeping the bottom free of glaze. Pieces stick if any glaze comes in contact with the kiln shelf during firing. Let glaze dry until it loses its sheen; then dip bowl into cobalt-blue glaze. This was done with the blue bowl shown opposite.

18: Form a 1.3 cm thick strip by rolling out clay on the working surface. Use the palms of your hands to do the rolling.

19: Loop a clay strip around to form a five-petalled flower. Press down where clay overlaps at the flower's centre.

20: Join flower shapes in bowl with slip. Each flower should touch others on at least three surfaces for strength.

21: Hold the bowl carefully as you lower it on to the prepared double-coil clay base. Bowl and base are joined with slip.

▶ Openwork ceramic bowls are coloured with white and blue glazes. Repeated dipping in glazes intensifies the colour.

▲ You can arrange the basic coiled-clay element to create many designs for sturdy coat hooks. Nail for hanging goes through open loop opposite the hook.

Ceramics
Coat Hooks

Familiarity with coil work will enable you to use the technique for other simple projects like these ceramic coat hooks. Work with clay soft enough to be easily rolled and coiled. To make a four-sided hook, start with four 30 cm long strips of clay rolled out to 1.3 cm in diameter. Mark the centre of each. Starting at one end of a strip, roll it to the centre to form a curl. Then roll from the other end until the curls touch. Make four curled segments, and place in position, as in photograph 22. Join the pieces with slip. Roll several small clay balls about 1.3 cm in diameter, and slip these on all touching joints, pressing each firmly into position as in photograph 23. Coils tend to unwind as they air-dry. The small spheres prevent unwinding and also give necessary strength at joints. Form the hook (photograph 24); place one end behind a curl, and slip the pieces together. Add a loop opposite the hook. Let dry; then bisque fire.

Ceramic hooks may be glazed in the same manner as the coiled bowl (see pages 58 and 59). First, dip in matt-white glaze. Let dry about 5 minutes; then dip in cobalt-blue glaze. Be sure to dip only the front two-thirds of the hook in glaze, so the back (which will rest on the kiln shelf) is glaze-free. Then glaze fire. All hooks pictured above were dipped into white or cobalt-blue glaze. Colour variations were achieved by re-dipping several times in one or both colours, or by dipping first in blue, then in white. For small amounts of surface colour, dip in one colour; paint on second sparingly.

22: Form curl shapes by rolling a strip towards the centre from both ends. As you finish each curled piece, place it in position with the others to make certain that all are similar in size.

23: Place slip between all touching edges and under each small clay sphere. Press the spheres firmly into position.

24: Cut 10 cm long rolled strip; double it; place in position for hook. Bend one end up into desired position.

25: Dip front of the coiled coat hook in matt-white glaze. Quantity of glaze is for dipping hooks and bowls on page 59.

These coil projects will give you a feeling for working with clay in this manner. They are by no means all you can do with clay coils. Experiment with thicker and thinner coils and different glaze colours. You can shape coils into cylinders, built around a biscuit tin; squares, built around a cardboard box; or curved forms, built over a bowl. Other projects might include sconces, trivets, and decorative picture frames.

CHEESES AND CHURNING
Natural Dairy Products

by Freda Baron Friedman

For thousands of years, people the world over have been making milk products that bear little or no resemblance to milk. Many of these are the result of fermentation. Others depend on churning or beating to convert them to their final state.

Making these foods at home, in much the way our ancestors did, is in itself interesting, and they are nutritionally valuable additions to the diet, as they are rich in vitamins and minerals. Since these home-made products do not contain any preservatives, natural-food purists consider them especially healthy. In any case, the flavours are fresh and excellent.

Basic equipment you will need to make cheeses and dairy products is found in most kitchens. You will need a cooking thermometer with calibrations from 20 to 50°C, and a few metres of cheesecloth or butter muslin. If you try making hard cheese then you will have to improvise a cheese press. A double-boiler and wooden spoons are also useful, but you can also use metal spoons and place a small pot set in a larger one to simulate a double boiler.

Kitchen Favourites and Celebrations
Yogurts and Sour Cream

Making yogurt is a good way to start learning cheesemaking. Though yogurt is not a cheese, the fermentation process responsible for yogurt is similar to the first step in making many soft cheeses. With the fermentation process you can make all sorts of dairy products, from cottage cheese to sour cream. The recipe for basic yogurt is given on page 64.

Yogurt depends on the growth of bacteria to form lactic acid. When milk is innoculated with one or more types of the yogurt bacteria, they begin to grow, forming lactic acid from the milk sugar, or lactose. The milk used differs from area to area, as do the bacteria. In this country, cow's milk is used; in Armenia, buffalo's or goat's milk; in Lapland, reindeer's or mare's milk. Flavour and consistency vary with the type of milk and the bacteria.

An historic food

Yogurt has been the diet of peasants and the delicacy of kings for more than four thousand years. Throughout history there have been rituals and rules about yogurt. In some countries, cultures of bacteria were passed down from generation to generation, as part of a girl's dowry. Legend tells that Genghis Khan fed his vast army on yogurt to give the men strength during their long marches through the Orient and Persia. Other legends have linked yogurt consumption with long life, virility, the restoration of thinning hair, and the treatment of ulcers and other stomach ailments. Persian women were reported to preserve the freshness of their skin by eating yogurt and using it as a facial cream. Even today, some people believe yogurt preserves the complexion and bleaches away freckles.

Fresh, home-made sweet butter, with jam and bread or biscuits, is not a treat confined to farmers; anyone can make the diary products pictured here. From left to right, front row, sweet butter and wax-coated, home-made firm cheese; back row, sour cream, yogurt soft cheese and cottage cheese.

Rich in nutrients

The rationale for these beliefs can be explained by yogurt's high protein, calcium, and lactic-acid content, which are supposed to be beneficial to the skin. While yogurt's beneficial values do remain heartily controversial, it nevertheless is a very popular food.

Basic yogurt is easy to make and is the basis for the dessert, salad dressing, soup, and soft cheese for which recipes are given on the opposite page. The bacteria are sensitive to temperature changes and the food they feed on. For best results, use fresh milk and fresh commercial yogurt as a starter. Aged yogurt used as a starter is less dependable.

Incubating yogurt

First, plan how to keep the milk mixture warm enough for the culture to develop—42 and 45°C—for 3 to 5 hours. Yogurt making appliances with temperature controls can be used, but you do not need one. An incubator can be easily improvised. You can use a vacuum flask; incubate the jar in a biscuit tin filled with cotton-wool as an insulator; or use an oven with a steady, low temperature control. Or use a Balkan method: Pour warm yogurt mixture into a casserole; cover; wrap with a blanket, and leave in a warm room overnight. By morning, the yogurt will be thick and ready for chilling.

Basic Yogurt

900 ml fresh milk
2 tablespoons powdered milk

1 tablespoon unflavoured
  commercial yogurt

Combine fresh milk and powdered milk in a heavy, stainless-steel or enamel pot. Over low heat and stirring constantly, bring slowly to boiling point. Pour mixture into a bowl to cool to about 26 to 30°C. Blend $\frac{1}{2}$ cup of the warm milk with the yogurt until mixture is smooth. Then add this mixture to the bowl of remaining warm milk. Pour into a preserving jar; cover, and keep warm, using one of the incubating methods described above. Incubate 3 to 5 hours—or overnight if you use blanket insulation. When the mixture is the consistency of thick cream, refrigerate it to chill before serving.

Makes four 225 g servings.

1: Pouring yogurt through a funnel helps to avoid spills when containers have narrow necks. Use any clean bottle with a neck wide enough for a spoon to be used for scooping out yogurt after it has set. The bottle should be equipped with a cap.

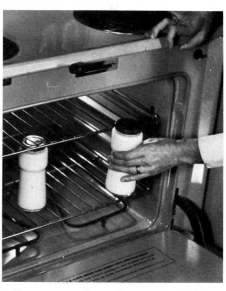

2: Your oven can be used as a yogurt maker if it will hold a temperature setting of 42 to 45°C steadily for several hours or overnight. If the oven heat goes above 46°C, it may kill the bacteria whose action makes the yogurt ferment.

Fresh-fruit Yogurt

900 ml fresh milk
2 tablespoons powdered milk
150 g fresh fruit or berries

1 tablespoon unflavoured
　commercial yogurt
Honey to taste

Scald fresh and powdered milk, and cool to 45°C. Incubate as directed for basic yogurt. Mix in the remaining ingredients. Refrigerate to chill before serving.
　Makes four 250 g servings.

Yogurt Salad Dressing

225 g basic yogurt
60 ml cider vinegar
1 medium onion, finely chopped
200 ml sunflower or vegetable oil

1 clove garlic, minced
150 g chopped celery leaves
75 g chopped parsley leaves

Blend all ingredients in an electric blender until smooth. Mix into chopped salad ingredients, or serve as a separate dressing.

Yogurt Tomato Soup

900 ml tomato juice
500 g basic yogurt

Pinch tarragon, preferably fresh
Lemon twists (optional)

Blend tomato juice, yogurt, and tarragon in an electric blender until smooth. Serve cold. Garnish each serving with a twist of lemon, if desired.
　Makes 6 to 8 servings.

Yogurt Soft Cheese

500 g basic yogurt
1 pinch sea salt

Finely chopped chives, onion, herbs,
　or caraway seeds to taste; or
　sliced fresh fruit

Pour surface whey from yogurt. Mix in sea salt, and put yogurt into a bag made of three 30 by 45 cm layers of cheesecloth. Hang bag over sink, and let drain overnight, or until yogurt is consistency of cream cheese. Refrigerate. If desired, add one of optional flavourings before serving as a spread. For a sweet flavour, blend or serve with fresh fruit slices. For a sharper cheese, use yogurt several days old.

Making sour cream

A simple method of making sour cream is to add 2 teaspoons lemon juice to each 150 ml single cream, and leave to stand for 30 minutes. An alternative recipe, below, uses a buttermilk culture. Try sweetened sour cream with fresh fruits and fruit salad: into 250 g of sour cream stir 1 tablespoon of granulated sugar. Plain sour cream (500 g) mixed with 1 small garlic clove, minced, makes a delicious dip for potato crisps.

Sour Cream

500 ml fresh double cream

5 teaspoons commercial cultured
　buttermilk

Thoroughly mix the cream and the buttermilk. (Shake buttermilk container well before measuring.) Pour mixture into a container that allows 3 or 4 cm of space at the top. Cover tightly, and shake thoroughly. Let stand in a warm place (20 to 30°C) for 24 hours. Or improvise an incubator, as in photograph 3. Refrigerate. Serve cold.

3: Incubator for sour cream is improvised from potful of warm water and thick, warm blanket. Place container of buttermilk and cream mixture in the warm water, and set pot on several thicknesses of the blanket. Wrap the rest of the blanket around pot and container, and leave overnight to incubate.

Kitchen Favourites and Celebrations
Cheeses

There are many legends about the discovery of cheesemaking, most of them with elements in common: Someone sets out on horseback on a journey, taking along some milk in a pouch made from a calf's stomach. After some time, the traveller finds that the milk has turned into a palatable sour curd.

Rennet, an enzyme from the lining of a calf's stomach, converts milk into curds and whey and is widely used in cheesemaking. The chief milk protein, casein, is curdled, or coagulated, by the enzyme action of rennet or pepsin, or by lactic acid produced by bacterial action, or by a combination of these.

Cheese is made from the milk of various animals, including cow, sheep, goat, buffalo, camel, ass, mare, llama, reindeer, yak, and zebu. As with yogurt, the flavour and consistency of cheese are determined by the type of milk and the conditions under which it is converted. And like wine, cheese has countless varieties. Basically, it is either soft or firm. Soft cheeses contain more moisture than firm cheeses. The home cheesemaker can easily make soft cheeses, many of which have a cottage-cheese base. The recipe on the opposite page is a good starting point.

Making cottage cheese
Soft cheeses such as cottage cheese can be made with rennet, yogurt, or cultured buttermilk as a starter. The recipe opposite uses rennet. This can

Before there were milk floats, milk vendors dispensed their product in city streets, from pails, as shown in this sketch of a milkman of the 1820s.

4: Cheesecloth bag twisted at the top serves as a press to force out watery, sour whey after the rennet-set milk curds have been heated.

5: Shifting curds around, by lifting the corners of the cheesecloth after whey has been removed, loosens them so water can rinse through the curds in next step.

6: Loosened curds in their cheesecloth bag are dipped in cold water and then drained as shown here. The cheesecloth around them is not squeezed.

7: Back in the colander after their water bath, the curds are gently worked with a wooden spoon to loosen and lighten the mass. Cottage cheese is now ready to eat.

be purchased as plain (not flavoured) junket rennet tablets, from Harrods in London; or cheese rennet liquid, from some health food shops or chemists. Both products are made by Hansens Laboratories, Basingstoke Road, Reading, Berks. Flavoured junket rennet liquid or tablets are not suitable.

Basic Cottage Cheese

2 plain junket rennet tablets, *or*
  7 drops liquid cheese rennet
50 ml cold water

1.8 litres skim milk
30 ml commercial cultured buttermilk

Crush and dissolve the tablet in the cold water. Combine skim milk and buttermilk. Heat milk mixture to 21°C. Add rennet solution, and stir well. Cover with a towel, and let stand at room temperature 12 to 18 hours, or until a smooth curd forms. Slowly heat curds, in a double-boiler top over hot water, until temperature reaches 45°C. Keep at this temperature 15 to 30 minutes, stirring about every 5 minutes so curds heat uniformly. When curds are firm, pour into a colander lined with cheesecloth, and let the whey drain off. Shift curds around by gently lifting the corners of the cloth. After whey has drained off, draw corners of cloth together, and immerse for about 2 seconds in cold water. Work curds with a wooden spoon to free them of any excess whey. Stir, chill. If cheese is dry, moisten with a little buttermilk. Add salt to taste.

8: Coeur à la creme—heart of cream—is shown with the heart-shaped wicker basket traditionally used to drain and mould this classic French dessert.

A cheese-based dessert

A delicious and simple dessert called coeur à la creme—heart of cream—can be made with yogurt soft cheese, page 65, or basic cottage cheese, above. Any fresh fruit may be used to garnish it. It is moulded in a heart-shaped basket.

Coeur à la Creme

900 g home-made cream cheese or
  cottage cheese
75 g basic yogurt

2 tablespoons granulated sugar
500 g fresh fruit, sliced
Granulated sugar to taste

Stir cheese, at room temperature, with yogurt and 2 tablespoons sugar until smooth. Line heart-shaped basket with cheesecloth; set on soup plate. Pack mixture into basket; drain and chill several hours, or overnight. To serve, unmould; garnish with fruit; sprinkle with sugar to taste.
  Makes 8 servings.

Cottage-Cheese Dip

500 g home-made cottage cheese
1 teaspoon celery seeds
1 teaspoon dill seeds
1 teaspoon caraway seeds

1 teaspoon chopped parsley
1 teaspoon chopped chives
Pinch paprika

Blend cottage cheese with celery, dill, and caraway seeds. Add parsley and chives. Chill for several hours. Before serving, sprinkle lightly with paprika. Serve with crackers or bread.

Making firm cheese

Firm cheeses usually travel better and last longer than soft cheeses, but they are more complex and time-consuming to make. Most people, except the adventurous, will not bother with home preparation. But if you would like to try making firm cheese, the recipe on page 68 is a basic one. When you are making firm cheese, remember that Marco Polo brought cheese similar to this one from the Orient to Europe. In the days before refrigeration and rapid transportation, it was one of the staple foods for long-distance travellers, because it was nutritious, kept well, and was easily carried.

9: Test curd for firm cheese to see if it is set enough. If curd slides down your finger instead of breaking cleanly over it, let curd set longer.

10: Cut curds with a long-bladed knife. Note that the pieces of curd here are quite small, about 1 cm in size. As you cut, avoid crushing the curds.

11: Place curds in the centre of a double layer of cheesecloth; then pull cloth corners together to form a cradle, and roll curds in it gently.

Basic process for firm cheese

The basic process for making firm cheese is similar to that for soft cheese, but firm cheese are usually made in large batches because they keep well and are aged several weeks before use. Sterilise equipment, and wash your hands before and during cheese making; firm cheese is liable to be contaminated by bacteria if you are not careful.

If you plan to make firm cheese often, you will want to have a cheese press. A simple one for small cheese can be constructed from two 20 by 30 cm pieces of 2 cm board, sanded. Join them with two 2.5 cm dowels, one centred through each end. With the lump of fresh cheese on the lower board, press the top board down, flattening the cheese evenly as you press out the remaining whey. As a substitute, set the cheese on a large, clean plate; set another plate on top, and weight—with an iron, for instance.

Basic Firm Cheese

8 litres fresh milk (preferably raw)	1 cup cold water
8 plain junket rennet tablets, *or* 5 ml liquid cheese rennet	2 tablespoons sea salt

Let 4 litres of the milk ripen overnight in a cool place (10 to 15°C). The following morning, add the other 4 litres. In a large, enamel or stainless steel pan, warm the milk to 30°C. Add tablets to the cold water, crush and stir until dissolved. Set pan in a larger vessel of warm water (31 to 32°C), away from draughts. Add rennet solution or liquid rennet, and stir thoroughly. Let stand undisturbed until a firm curd forms—about 30 to 45 minutes. Test firmness by carefully putting a finger into the curd at an angle and lifting it. If curd breaks cleanly over your finger, it is ready to cut. If not, let it set 15 to 20 minutes longer.

Remove pan from larger vessel, and cut curd into 1 cm cubes. Use a knife with a blade long enough to cut through to bottom of pot without the handle touching the curd. Stir curd cubes carefully but thoroughly with wooden spoon about 15 minutes; use long, slow movements so curds are not crushed. Place pan in a larger pan with water (creating a double-boiler effect), and heat slowly, raising curds' temperature about 1 degree every 5 minutes until it reaches 30°C. Stir with a wooden spoon to keep curds from sticking together. Remove from heat when curds start to hold their shape and readily fall apart when held, but not squeezed, together.

Stir every 5 minutes for about 1 hour (that's right!) to keep curds from sticking. Leave them in the whey until the mass becomes so firm that a handful of pieces, pressed together, will shake apart easily. Put the curds on a double layer of 1 m square cheesecloth, and pull corners of cloth together. Swing gently, letting curds roll back and forth so whey drains without squeezing. Sprinkle curds with half of sea salt, and mix well with wooden spoon. Sprinkle on remaining sea salt, and mix in by hand.

Tie cheesecloth so curds form a ball; hang up, and let whey drip for 45 minutes. Remove cheesecloth; fold it into a rectangular bandage, 8 cm by 1 m, and wrap tightly around the ball. With your hands, press down on ball until top and bottom are flat. Put three or four layers of cheesecloth under and over the cheese. Place in press; adjust pieces of wood; put a heavy object on the press; leave overnight. Turn; press overnight again.

Remove cheese from the press, and remove cheesecloth wrapping. Let stand in a warm room (21 to 23°C) for 6 hours while rind forms and dries out. Then coat with hot, melted paraffin wax. Holding cheese with tongs, dip one half and then the other. Or paint on melted wax with a basting brush. An alternative to wax coating is rubbing vegetable oil into the cheese. Ripen in a cool place (10 to 18°C) 3 to 4 weeks; turn two or three times a week.

Kitchen Favourites and Celebrations
Churning

Churning or agitating is the process that makes fat globules in milk unite—the end product is butter. The process dates back to about 2000 B.C., when churning was achieved by filling skin pouches with milk and throwing them back and forth, or letting them swing over the backs of trotting horses. The butter made then was used most often as an ointment for the bath, a medicine or lamp oil.

As butter became a staple food, hand churns for the dairy were devised—rotating, swinging, or rocking barrels or boxes and cylindrical vessels, equipped with plungers or dashers. Today, butter is made with electric churns. Churning time depends on the composition of the butterfat; the temperature, acidity, and richness of the cream; the speed and motion of the churn; and the size of the fat globules.

Butter's natural colour, which ranges from pale yellow to deep gold, is derived from the carotene in the fodder the milk-giving animal—the cow or some other animal—has eaten. In this country, cream from cow's milk is generally used in making butter; but in some countries, cream from the milk of goats, sheep, and mares is converted into butter.

All butter, when it is freshly made, is sweet. Salt is added to butter as a preservative and for flavour. You can easily make your own fresh, sweet butter using an electric mixer. When heavy cream is whipped long enough, it is transformed into little round, yellow globules of fat swimming in a bowl of whey. When it is beaten for another minute or so, the grainy, yellow lumps join together to form a ball of butter.

You can follow the recipe below to make a variety of flavoured butters. Just beat in honey or salt to taste, or add herbs, spices, or other flavourings.

Flavoured Butter

250 ml heavy cream

½ to 1 teaspoon salt, herbs, spices, or other flavourings

In a bowl whip cream with an electric mixer at medium speed until butter separates from whey. Pour off whey; beat in flavouring. Makes 150 g.

Making fresh mayonnaise

A churning process with a different principle behind it produces a delicious fresh mayonnaise. By beating mustard into the yolks of eggs, with a little salt and vinegar or lemon juice, you create a chemical change that allows the yolks to absorb quantities of oil, rather as rice absorbs water when it is boiled. The result is a creamy, golden mayonnaise with a unique flavour. It is an excellent dressing for meat salads, cold vegetables, and potato salad. Sweetened with 1 teaspoon granulated sugar and mixed half-and-half with whipped cream, it is delicious with jellied salad rings.

Mayonnaise

1 teaspoon salt
½ teaspoon dry mustard
2 egg yolks

2 tablespoons vinegar or lemon juice
350 ml salad oil
Pinch cayenne

In a medium bowl, mix salt, mustard, egg yolks, and 1 teaspoon vinegar. With electric mixer at high speed, beat in ¼ of the oil, a few dribbles at a time. Add the remaining vinegar and the cayenne. Slowly beat in the remaining oil. Keep refrigerated. Makes 400 ml.

12: Adding egg yolks to salt and mustard is first step in making fresh mayonnaise. Stir mixture with a wooden spoon until the ingredients form a smooth paste. Then stir in 1 teaspoon of the vinegar.

13: With electric mixer at high speed, beat the egg mixture while dribbling in ¼ of the oil, a few drops at a time. Next, beat in remaining vinegar; then slowly dribble in remaining oil.

14: Garnish with a few tarragon leaves, and the finished mayonnaise is ready to be served. It has a rich golden colour and a thick, creamy texture and holds its shape like whipped cream.

CHRISTMAS CELEBRATIONS
All through the House

by Elvin McDonald

Christmas is that warm and wonderful time of year when we renew ties with old friends and exchange sentiments of good will. True to this ideal, we give and receive gifts on the big day, but I think the real enjoyment of Christmas lies in its preparation. This can be a time of genuine family togetherness and group effort. Instead of the usual last-minute pressure of buying gifts and manufactured decorations, why not return to the Christmas of tradition—strings of bright red berries, hand-made ornaments, and wreaths of fresh pine? With a little effort and planning, you can bring the warmth of an authentically traditional Christmas into your home.

Many of our Christmas traditions—the use of evergreens included—originated as part of ancient holiday rituals. The Celts believed that evergreens placed over the entrances to their homes had the power to ward off evil spirits, and they placed sprigs of holly and mistletoe indoors as symbols of eternal life. The Romans raised an evergreen bough to celebrate the winter solstice. At the same time of year, they celebrated the feast of Saturn, and the New Year that followed, with banquets, exchanges of gifts, and the use of decorative greenery and torches.

The custom of bringing an evergreen tree indoors originated in the 15th century in western Germany, where forests of fir trees abounded. The decorated Christmas tree became popular around 1500 in the area of the upper river Rhine. It was adorned with paper ornaments and edible decorations, such as apples and sugar, and in Scandinavia and other parts of northern Europe, trees are still decorated in this manner.

Living Christmas trees

I prefer a living tree for Christmas. With its roots protected, it can later be planted in your garden or potted for your terrace. Best for in-ground planting, in areas where needled evergreens prosper, are firs, pines, spruces, and upright yews (*Taxus baccata*). For container planting, choose a pine or upright yew. Hemlocks are not likely to survive a stay indoors.

Buy from a reliable nursery and make sure the tree roots have not been boiled. Test a tree's health by pulling its needles; if they come off easily, the tree is too dry. Avoid trees with branch yellowing, especially near the trunks. If you live in northern areas, it is a good idea to dig the planting hole in autumn before the ground freezes. Fill the hole with straw, or cover with a tarpaulin. Later, drag the heavy root ball on the tarpaulin for easy moving. When you bring the tree home, store it outdoors with roots wrapped

In the inset photograph are colourful ribbons and confectionery wreaths; instructions are on page 80. In the large photograph are handcrafted tree ornaments. Instructions for the painted balls and the tasselled-fringe ball, far right, are on page 75.

Figure A: To protect a live tree against dryness, spray with anti-desiccant from a garden store. Keep balled roots moist in a tub or a large basin.

in a blanket. Indoors, do not stand the tree near a fireplace or other heat source. To keep the earth surrounding the roots moist, place the tree in a wooden tub, or large basin, with a few centimetres of water in it at all times. Wedge some kindling wood under edges of the root ball to hold the tree securely upright. If your nurseryman has not already done so, spray the tree with an anti-desiccant (see figure B, opposite). This is a transparent plastic coating that will help to keep the needles green and moisture-filled.

Cut Christmas trees
If you prefer a cut Christmas tree, bear in mind these recommendations for its handling:
☐ Select a fresh, green tree with resilient needles and strong scent.
☐ Saw off the butt end of the tree (see figure B, opposite).
☐ Keep the butt end standing in a container of water during the entire time the tree is indoors.

1: Lights go on tree first. Begin at top, and wind around and down. Before hanging, plug in to check for loose or dead bulbs.

2: Push bead up. This will tighten wires around branch. These are small, white lights that use little electricity.

3: After covering tree, plug in lights; adjust spacing; then secure each light by looping wire around branch, as shown.

Garlands of popcorn and red berries, folded-paper stars, patchwork balls, sweets, fruit, and real carnations make this a sumptuous, yet traditional, Christmas tree.

B

Figure B: For cut tree, saw off trunk at least 2.5 cm above original cut.
Position in a sturdy stand according to directions; add water every day or two.

☐ Be sure the tree is well supported and is away from fireplaces, radiators, television sets, and other sources of heat.
☐ Never use lighted candles or other open flames on or near the tree.
☐ Never use worn, frayed wires. Check lights and connections.
☐ Do not use combustible decorations or inflammable reflectors for lights.
☐ Avoid overloading electric circuits. Do not leave accumulations of wrapping paper or electrical toys under the tree.

   To make your cut tree more fire-resistant, add 250 g of borax and 110 g of boric-acid crystals or powder to 4.5 litres of warm water. Mix, and apply the solution to the tree with a mist-type sprayer.

Designs and Decorations
Patchwork Christmas Balls

by Stephen Barany

These patchwork Christmas tree balls are easy to make and very lightweight. To make them, you will need as many foam balls as you wish, in various sizes (available at hobby shops); medium-weight florist's wire; wire cutters to cut the wire (or you can use side-cutting pliers or old scissors); ribbons or scraps of cloth patterned in assorted checks, stripes, and polka dots; sharp scissors; enough ribbon to make a few squares and a bow for each ball; and some white glue.

Cut a piece of florist's wire as long as the foam ball's diameter, plus 20 cm for securing and hanging. Push it through the centre of the ball. Form a loop at one end (see photograph 6), for hanging the ball. Leave about 2.5 cm of excess wire at the other end. Bend this, and push the end back into the foam to secure the wire. Cut the ribbons or cloth scraps into roughly 2.5 cm squares. Apply glue to the backs, and press squares on to the ball. Tie a ribbon bow around the base of the wire loop.

4: Here are glue, fabric scraps, ribbon, and foam ball needed to make a patchwork ornament. It will be most attractive if you use fabrics of different patterns but of the same colour or colour combination.

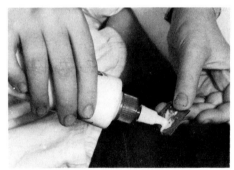

5: Apply glue, and then smear it over back of square with your finger. Press and smooth the square on to the foam ball.

6: Apply squares at random, and overlap slightly. Use some squares cut from the ribbon for the bow (see photograph below).

This tree ornament recalls the charm of a patchwork quilt. It is easy to make—something the whole family, including the children, can do.

Designs and Decorations
Hand-made Christmas Balls

To make the tasselled-fringe ornament on the right in the colour photograph on page 71, you will need a 15 cm foam ball, a small, round mirror, white glue, scissors, a scrap of felt, 1 metre of gold braid, straight pins, 1 metre of tasselled fringe, a garland of gold and a garland of pink tiny balls, bead-headed pins, large sequins, and florist's wire for hanging.

Glue and press mirror on to ball to flatten foam. Cut a 5 cm diameter circle of felt, and glue to side of ball directly opposite mirror. Wrap and pin strip of gold braid around mirror (photograph 7). Wrap and pin three rows of fringe around ball centre. Thread bead-headed pins with gold garland balls in pairs, and position pins to form circle around centre of ball at fringe. Pin gold braid so it covers edge of felt and area between felt and fringe (photograph 8). Thread bead-headed pins with single pink ball and sequin, and position pins to form circle at outer edge of gold braid around mirror. Thread bead-headed pins with one gold ball; pin around mirror edge.

To make one of the painted balls in the photograph on page 71, you will need a glass or plastic Christmas ball, a tin of artist's canvas primer (sold at art-supply shops), two or three artist's paintbrushes, a felt marker, tubes of acrylic paint in various colours, and clear varnish spray.

Pull off ball's cap and hanger. Paint with primer (photograph 9), and let dry. Draw design with marker (photograph 10), and paint with acrylic paint (photograph 11). Spray with varnish. Replace cap and hanger.

7: Wrap gold braid around mirror. As you pin braid down, overlap edges slightly so white foam will not show through.

8: Applying braid around circle of felt. Overlap felt slightly. When finished, pierce ball with wire for hanging.

9: For painted ornament, prime the ball with artist's canvas primer (gesso). Your overlay design of acrylic paint will adhere permanently to this base coat.

10: For a guideline, draw a design of your choosing with a felt-tip marking pen. Any mistakes in design execution can later be corrected by covering with acrylic paint.

11: Use bright colours to fill in design. Experiment with geometric shapes. Allow paint to dry thoroughly, and spray the ball with clear varnish.

75

Designs and Decorations
Natural and Paper Trims

Natural and edible items make charming decorations for your tree. This detail shows gumdrops, sugar canes, apples, a pear, a berry garland, and a carnation. Small, brightly coloured toys, such as the red-and-white drum shown, are also appropriate ornaments.

12: To keep flower fresh, cut stem short, and slide into a water-filled tube. Check water level daily; refill as needed.

On the tree pictured in colour on page 73, I used pink and red carnations, berry and popcorn garlands, apples, pears, and crab apples, foil-wrapped sweets, and large gumdrops. To decorate your tree this way, you will need, in addition to the natural materials, florist's wire and some old scissors or side-cutting pliers to cut it; a spool of thread and a sewing needle (a needle and length of thread for each member of the family will make stringing popcorn and berries a pleasant group activity); and a plastic watering tube or vial (photograph 12) for each of your fresh flowers. These tubes are sold at florist's shops.

Confectionery
The reflective quality of the foil wrapping on sweets makes them ideal tree decorations. Thread seven or eight of them on some florist's wire; twist ends of wire together, forming a circle. If you work gently, the wrapping will not break apart. Attach a wire loop for hanging the ring of sweets.

Gumdrops or sugared fruit jellies (see colour photograph, left) also make colourful ornaments. Thread three or four gumdrops, through the bottom and out the top, on a length of florist's wire. Bend the wire at the bottom of the gumdrop column to secure it. Form a loop with the wire at the top to hang the column on your tree.

Berry and popcorn garlands
A garland of red berries, or berries alternating with pieces of popcorn, is a Christmas decoration idea which originated in Colonial America. It is still popular in the United States today, where they use cranberries; in this country, try holly, ash or Cotoneaster berries for a cheap and cheerful garland. But warn children not to eat them.

Make a large bowl or two of popcorn at least two weeks before you intend to string it, so it has plenty of time to soften. Leave the popcorn in the kitchen; the steam from cooking will ensure its softness.

String two types of garland—one solely of berries and the other alternating two pieces of popcorn with two berries. Use no more than a 1 metre length of double thread at a time; longer thread is unwieldy. Thread the needle, and knot the ends of the thread with a double knot. Pierce each berry and piece of popcorn with the needle, and slide it on to the thread. Do not fill the entire thread; leave 15 cm between the needle and the last berry or piece of popcorn. Cut this thread from the needle, and tie it to one of the tree's uppermost branches. Wind the garland down and around the tree, draping it as you go. Start the second string where the first one ends, and continue in the same manner with more garlands until you reach the bottom of the tree.

Fruit and flowers
Apples, pears, and crab apples are fine tree decorations and can be secured easily to the tree. Simply pierce them through the length of their cores with florist's wire, bend the wire's bottom end, and push it into the fruit. Wind the top end of the wire around one of the larger branches or close to the tree trunk on a smaller branch.

You can decorate your tree with whatever fresh flowers you wish, so long as you provide watering tubes (see photograph 12) for all of them and put the flowers into the tubes before you attach them to the tree. The flowers will last from Christmas Eve to New Year's Day if the tubes are kept filled with water. Secure a tube to the tree by placing it upright against a branch, with the flower facing out, and wrapping tube and branch with florist's wire (or you can use florist's tape). Do not cover the tube's rubber stopper.

Paper star. A sheet of paper 18 cm square makes a star 16.5 by 18 cm. Use any size paper, so long as it is square. For the best-looking star, use foil wrapping paper that is white on one side. Begin by folding paper in half from top to bottom. Open, and fold in half from left to right, Open; turn over, and follow photographs.

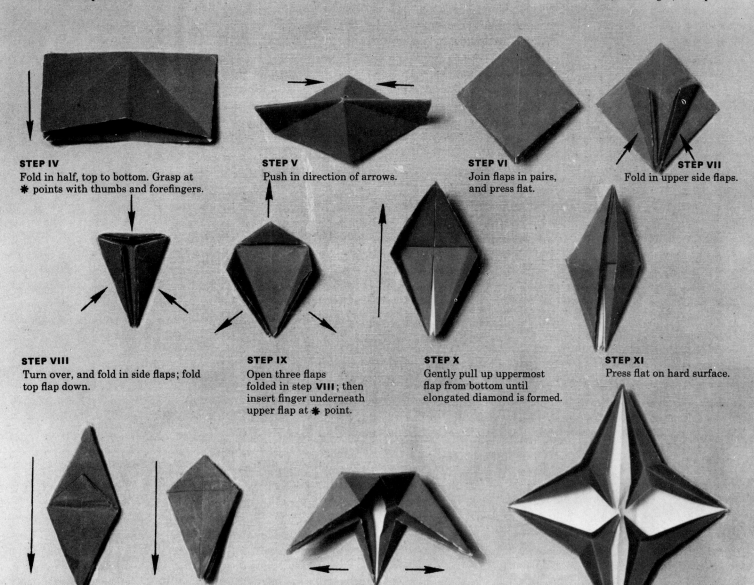

STEP I
Fold corner to point where two folds cross.

STEP II
Fold in all corners in same manner.

STEP III
Fold in half, left to right, and open.

STEP IV
Fold in half, top to bottom. Grasp at
✳ points with thumbs and forefingers.

STEP V
Push in direction of arrows.

STEP VI
Join flaps in pairs,
and press flat.

STEP VII
Fold in upper side flaps.

STEP VIII
Turn over, and fold in side flaps; fold
top flap down.

STEP IX
Open three flaps
folded in step **VIII**; then
insert finger underneath
upper flap at ✳ point.

STEP X
Gently pull up uppermost
flap from bottom until
elongated diamond is formed.

STEP XI
Press flat on hard surface.

STEP XII
Turn over; repeat steps
VII-X, and fold down
top flap.

STEP XIII
Turn over, and
fold down top flap as
in step **XII**.

STEP XIV
Grasp inner flaps at ✳ points, and pull
apart in direction of arrows until . . .

STEP XV
Completed star
snaps into shape.

Paper Folding and Cutting
Christmas Gift Wraps

This Christmas, be clever and creative in your gift wrapping. On the left are some ideas, and below are basic instructions for wrapping a gift box.

Interesting package trimmings that hint at what might be inside are easy to improvise. Top, glued-on scoop and raw rice. Bottom, wooden utensils and basket.

Wraps for children include, left, fabric wrapping with small stuffed animal taped on and, right, pages of cartoons from coloured comics which no child can resist.

Toy soldiers stand guard over a foil-wrapped package, decorated with a small plastic box and paper flowers.

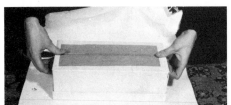

13: Place box, lid down, on paper. Centre it, and be sure paper is large enough to wrap around box and overlap 2.5 cm.

15: Bring up the other side of the paper, and overlap the first. Fold the edge under, and tape it to the paper beneath.

17: Fold down the top paper flap, and tape it. Be sure sides of paper under flap are smoothed closely against box.

19: For something different in ribbon trimming, wrap a length of wide ribbon around box, and tape two ends together.

14: Bring one side of the paper up and over; fold the edge under for neatness, and tape to the box along the fold.

16: Push in sides of end paper, squaring it neatly against box. End-paper length should be slightly less than box depth.

18: Fold over the edge of the bottom flap. Then fold the flap against the box, and tape it securely along its edge.

20: Over the wide ribbon, wrap a narrow one of co-ordinating or contrasting colour, and tape two ends together.

Greenery and Growing Things
Wheat-and-flower Wreath

by Maria Wizmur

Using wheat or straw trimmed with dried flowers is a centuries-old Christmas tradition in the Slavic countries of eastern Europe. These natural materials—used to make the wreath shown here and the tree in the colour photograph on page 82—will add a pleasant rustic and international touch to your Christmas.

To make the wreath shown in the colour photograph, right, you will need a 50 cm diameter foam wreath form; 2.5 kilos of dried wheat stalks (about 600 stalks); florist's wire; a pair of pliers; three dozen U-shaped florist's pins, or use florist's wire, cut and bent to a U-shape; large and small silk poppies and dried daisies, poppy seed pods, buttercups, and delphiniums. Poppies are one of the few flowers that cannot be dried. Purchase the others already dried, or you can use flowers you have dried. All these materials are available at your florist's, or he can get them for you at a flower market. The wheat could be obtained quite easily at harvest time in the country. Follow this step-by-step procedure to make the wheat-and-flower wreath:

Cut the tops of all the wheat stalks to 23 cm lengths.

Bunch three or four stalks together, and secure them with a twist of florist's wire. Use pliers to bend the wire tightly around the wheat stalks.

Attach the stalks to the wreath form by inserting the wire tightly into the foam at a sharp angle, so the stalks lie almost flat (see photograph 21). Cover the entire form, including the sides, this way. Do not cover the back. Make sure that all the stalks lean in the same direction around the wreath.

Insert U-shape pins wherever they are needed (photograph 22).

Attach lengths of wire to all the dried or silk flowers you are using, and push the wire through the wheat stalks and into the foam. Less wire will be needed if you gather three or four flowers into bunches and use one twist of wire for each bunch.

Attach wire to each poppy seed pod, and insert it into the foam.

The tree on page 82 is made the same way as the wreath, but on a 90 cm high foam Christmas-tree form. Again, the wheat stalks are inserted at a sharp angle. In imitation of the branches of a real tree, they should lie almost flat, with their tops downwards. Trim with flowers and seed pods in the same manner as the wreath. Tiny wooden toys or figures, if you have some, are also appropriate for this kind of tree.

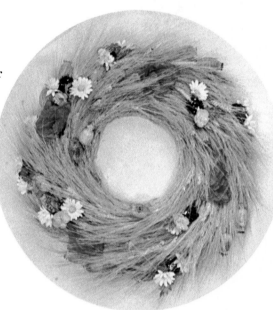

This traditional Slavic wreath is made of wheat stalks and dried flowers.

21: Insert the wire, with the stalks attached, in to the foam at a sharp angle. Place them close to one another, and overlap stalks generously, as shown.

22: Inserting a U-shape pin. After you have covered the form, use pins to gather and hold any stray stalks and generally shape and tidy the wreath.

A little girl works intently on her gumdrop wreath. She places gumdrops on the form as close together as possible.

Designs and Decorations
Confectionery Wreaths

A child's fantasy could not conjure up anything more sumptuous than a wreath generously covered with all kinds of sweets. This little Christmas project is something children can do—if they are not overcome by the temptation to eat all the materials. With a little supervision, they can make the wreaths in the photograph below or create their own variations.

To make these wreaths, you will need three 25 cm diameter foam wreath forms (available at a florist's or a craft shop); two boxes of flat, wooden toothpicks (rounded ones tend to fall out of the foam); 500 g each of gumdrops, fruit jellies, foil-wrapped sweets, marzipan shaped and coloured like fruit, and soft glacé cherries; and ribbon for bows.

Break some toothpicks in half. Push a sweet on to the end of a toothpick half, and insert the rest of the toothpick all the way into the foam. For each wreath, cover the entire form, except the space for a bow.

Cheerful wreath designers display their confectionery wreaths. Any kind of soft sweets could be used, but beware of chocolate which could melt.

Greenery and Growing Things
Mantelpiece Wreath

Preserve a tradition of Christmases past by fashioning a wreath of fresh greenery. You will need a wire coat hanger; two dozen 15 to 30 cm long evergreen branches (you can cut them from a tree or shrub in your garden, or buy a taller Christmas tree than needed and use the lower branches); a spool of medium-weight florist's wire and a wire cutter (see materials listed on page 74); scissors; crab apples; and two metres of wide ribbon for a bow.

Figure C: Use florist's wire and wire hanger to make greenery wreath. Hanger need not be bent into perfect circle. Leave hook on hanger so wreath can be hung easily.

The hearth is a Christmas gathering place, where a wreath will be admired. Wreath instructions are given here.

Bend coat hanger as shown in figure C. Bunch two or three branches; wind wire around their bases. Begin winding wire on coat hanger frame (figure C, left). Place branch bunch on frame; wind wire around base of branches and frame (figure C, centre). Try not to catch upper part of branches; they should be loose. Continue around frame (figure C, right). Make sure all branches lie in same direction. When hanger is covered, cut wire, and trim sprigs, if necessary, with scissors. Add crab apples, as pictured. Pierce each with wire, and twist wire into wreath. To make the bow, see figure D.

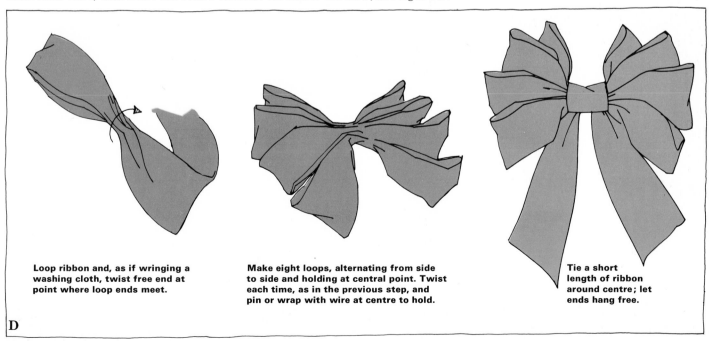

Loop ribbon and, as if wringing a washing cloth, twist free end at point where loop ends meet.

Make eight loops, alternating from side to side and holding at central point. Twist each time, as in the previous step, and pin or wrap with wire at centre to hold.

Tie a short length of ribbon around centre; let ends hang free.

Figure D: Follow these steps to make a wreath bow. Use two metres of wide ribbon. Attach to wreath with wire.

Christmas Buffet

A tree-trimming party the Sunday before Christmas is a cheerful occasion for celebration. A tempting buffet, with hot mulled wine (wassail bowl) and cold eggnog, hot mincemeat pie and rich fruit cake, will amply reward the decorators. Fruit cake and mincemeat can be prepared weeks ahead. The recipes here make four large pies and four cakes.

Mulled Wine with Cranberries

4 litres dry red wine	300 ml brandy (optional)
$\frac{1}{2}$ teaspoon ground mace	4 cinnamon sticks
6 teaspoons honey	3 thin slices lemon
150 g cranberries	3 thin slices orange

In a 3-litre saucepan, heat the wine, mace, honey, and half the cranberries until almost boiling. Stir in brandy. Pour into large serving bowl.
Float lemon and orange slices and remaining cranberries on top. Stir with cinnamon sticks; then float the sticks in the wine. Makes 16 to 20 servings.

Felt-covered table pinned with ribbons bears traditional treats: mulled wine, fruit cake, mincemeat pie, eggnog. Wheat-tree directions are on page 79; keep away from candles.

Eggnog

500 ml heavy cream
6 eggs
1 teaspoon vanilla extract
4 tablespoons sugar
½ teaspoon ground mace

300 ml brandy (optional)
2 litres cold, whole milk
Grated rind of 1 orange
⅛ teaspoon nutmeg

Whip cream until stiff. Beat eggs, vanilla, sugar, mace, and brandy until thick. Stir in milk. Pour into a large serving bowl. Stir in whipped cream. Sprinkle with grated orange rind and nutmeg. Makes 16 servings.

Four Fruit Cakes

700 g vegetable shortening
900 g sugar
900 g pastry flour
1 teaspoon each allspice,
   cinnamon, baking soda
14 eggs
1 teaspoon almond extract
1.8 kg mixed, candied fruits

500 g each stoned dates,
   glacé cherries, angelica
1.4 kg sultanas
500 g each chopped walnuts,
   slivered blanched almonds
150 ml rum or brandy
225 g each walnut halves, angelica,
   glacé cherries

In a very large salad bowl or 5 litre bowl, cream shortening with sugar. Into another bowl, sift flour with allspice, cinnamon, and soda. In another large bowl, beat eggs and almond extract until thick. Beat egg and flour mixtures alternately into shortening mixture. On floured board, chop candied fruits, dates, 500 g cherries and angelica; mix with raisins. Chop 500 g walnuts coarsely. Mix fruits, chopped walnuts, and almonds; beat into mixture. Mix in rum. Turn into 4 greased, floured, 18 or 20 cm cake tins. Decorate with glacé cherries, angelica squares, and walnut halves. Bake in pre-heated 140°C oven, Mark 1, for 2 hours, or until skewer inserted in centres comes out clean. Cool in pans on rack 2 or 3 hours. Turn out; wrap in cheesecloth rinsed in rum; seal with foil. Makes 4 cakes. For 2 cakes or 1 large cake, halve the above ingredients and use same method.

Mincemeat

340 g white beef suet
340 g each currants, raisins,
   sultanas
340 g peeled, chopped apple
225 g each chopped candied
   orange and lemon peel

225 g blanched almonds
30 g blanched bitter almonds
⅛ teaspoon each cinnamon,
   mace, salt, white pepper
225 ml brandy
Grated rind 1 lemon
Strained juice 1 lemon

Put suet through fine blade of mincer twice. In large bowl, combine suet with currants, raisins, and apple. Finely chop candied peels and almonds; add to suet mixture. Combine cinnamon, mace, salt, and pepper; add to suet mixture. Bake, in ovenproof dish, in pre-heated 150°C, Mark 2, oven for 30 minutes. Remove from oven; stir in brandy, lemon rind and juice. Seal in a 4 or 5 litre casserole or bowl. Will keep in refrigerator 2 weeks, or if frozen, indefinitely. Makes enough for 4 big pies. Use quarter or half amounts of ingredients for 1 or 2 pies.

Mincemeat Pie

Pastry dough for double crust, 23 cm wide
Cold milk
About 750 g mincemeat

Fit bottom crust into 23 cm pie plate. Fill with mincemeat. Cover with top crust; slash, and brush with cold milk. Bake in pre-heated 180°C, Mark 4, oven for 45 minutes. One pie makes 8 to 10 servings.

COLLAGES AND ASSEMBLAGES
Art from Scraps

by Barbara Auran-Wrenn

If you have ever made a valentine by pasting up bits of lace and coloured paper, you have made a collage. The technique is centuries-old, and can be traced back to the folk art of making paper cut-outs. Until the turn of this century, it was charmingly naïve and unselfconscious. In Victorian times, elaborate pictures of bouquets and landscapes were constructed of bristly horsehair. Scrapbooks of the period were also a form of collage, as were hand-made children's books stitched with soft, muslin pages, then pasted with pictures from catalogues and magazines. People saved ornate cigar bands and glued them in fancy borders on boxes. Another example is encountered in paintings on which actual objects, such as seashells and butterflies, were pasted to represent themselves. Perhaps the artist used this device hoping to fool the eye, or to hide lack of skill.

This collage includes waves cut from coloured tissue paper, illustrations from children's picture books, old postcards, an old blueprint, decorated cardboard poker chips, a section of folding ruler, and a cloth watchband. All are glued to a wooden board that, with a valance at the top, came from a timber-yard scrap pile. To see an example of a free-standing sculptural assemblage, turn to page 92.

From painting to collage

Modern collage began around 1910 when Picasso pasted a piece of newspaper on a drawing. The impact of this creation was enormous and indicated that flat, formal painting was no longer adequate for any creative need. Beginning in 1919, a German artist, Kurt Schwitters, developed collage into a medium as important as painting. From rubbish dumps, dustbins and pavements, he gathered the cast-off materials that went into his little pictures, and transformed his ragged scraps into an orderly world. Because of Schwitters and others like him, including observant photographers, we have become aware of the natural collages of papers stuck to the pavement by the rain; parts and pieces of things discarded and useless. Modern derivatives of this art form are pure-paper collages like those on the right, and on pages 86 and 87.

From collages to assemblages

Within a few years, Picasso's experiment with paper pasted on a drawing had been expanded to include the addition of real objects. When a collage is made with three-dimensional objects, it is called an assemblage or a construction. With the invention of assemblages, virtually all limitations on creative materials disappeared. Even the concept of working within a picture frame ceased to be important. Today, the words collage and assemblage are becoming almost synonymous, since it is difficult to say where one ends and the other begins. The more purely structural forms, like those on pages 92 and 93, are called assemblages, but many collages now contain some three-dimensional objects.

Collages and assemblages, hovering as they do between painting and sculpture, art and craft, offer the unskilled craftsman a point of entry into the fine arts. Since the objects are merely collected and fastened to a surface, usually by glueing, pegging, or nailing, no special training is required in the techniques of drawing perspectives, curves, circles, and the other phenomena of representational and non-representational painting. In fact, much that an artist working with paint attempts to reproduce on a flat surface is inherent in the dimension, colour, and form of an object fastened to a surface.

Materials and inspiration

Since the techniques used in making collages and assemblages are simple—glueing, pegging, and nailing—the art lies in the selection and arrangement of materials, and it must be personal. You will not want to reproduce exactly some other artist's painting. Training and experience teach one an awareness of the potential of objects. For Schwitters, the pavement and rubbish dump furnished useful materials. The collages and assemblages on the next pages indicate some of the sources of inspiration for contemporary artists.

For the artist, a collage usually begins with a series of questions. Standing in a timber-yard, or looking at a magazine or old greeting cards, the artist broods: will bits of wood, fixed to a board, make a statement, evoke a mood? Will one picture, added to another, become something else? What will happen if different textures and shapes are treated this way? Bit by bit, an idea for a finished work begins to simmer. It is something like the thoughts that go through your mind when you doodle.

In looking at the discards around us for ways in which to change and combine or re-combine them, many qualities attract us. We consider the object's design and colour; we notice its textures—surfaces are smooth or rough, bright or dull. Some things appear fragile and delicate, others massive and heavy. Much of the excitement of making collages comes from being able to combine these different qualities in a variety of ways to tell a story, state a theme, evoke a mood, startle or please with imaginative new symbiotic or suggestive effects. Collages are truly an art form that is unfettered by conventional materials and formal techniques. What we often discover in making collages and assemblages is our personal reaction to things around us. In creating, we discover ourselves.

A Christmas card in the collage technique called "pure-paper" has no three-dimensional elements at all. It is made of cut-outs gathered from magazines and from old greeting cards. Its creator has used a combination of the two methods—glue-under and glue-over, illustrated on pages 86 and 87—to produce this work.

COLLAGES AND ASSEMBLAGES

Designs and Decorations
Pure-paper Collage

by Carol Wald
The two main techniques used in collages are illustrated in the colour
pictures on these pages: the glue-over technique and the glue-under technique.

Materials and tools:
To cut, sharp artist's knife and blades, straight-edge ruler; to cut on, heavy
chipboard, about 55 by 75 cm; to outline positions of pictures, soft lead
pencil; to glue, rubber cement; to mount finished collages, 30 by 35 cm white
board sheets; to file potential collage pictures, manila folders.

Your picture collection should include lots of large colour pictures from
magazines, greeting cards, postcard reproductions. File according to subject:
people, places, objects, backgrounds, and so on. To make a good collage, you
need as wide a selection of pictures as possible.

1: Use a sharp-pointed artist's knife to
cut cleanly when preparing pictures for
collages. Change the blade as soon
as it dulls. Cutting is done on chipboard.

2: With sharp lead pencil, outline on the
base picture the position of cut-out
pictures selected to be glued under
or over the base picture.

Glue-over technique of collage begins with the selection of a large picture. This will be
the base on which a fanciful assortment of cut-out objects is placed, as here.

86

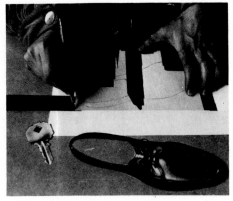

3: Use a ruler to centre base picture squarely on white board; pencil-mark corners. Glue this picture to the board before glueing on secondary pictures.

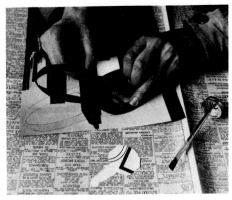

4: To glue pictures, completely cover with a light coat of rubber cement all surfaces (including edges) to be joined. Let dry one minute before glueing down.

Glue-under technique of collage creates a picture in which you view one image through another. Here, the flower picture is glued under cut-out portions of the head.

To make a glue-over collage, begin by selecting about 15 appealing pictures of objects. The choice should be as random as possible. Cut out carefully, as in photograph 1. Select a full-page picture, and place the cut-outs on it anywhere you like. Experiment with positioning, and have fun with your ideas. Following the instructions for photographs 2 to 4, outline the position of the objects on the base picture; then mount the base picture on white board, and glue on objects selected.

A glue-under collage is made in the same way. Select the top picture first; cut away the unwanted portions; then slide other pictures under the cut-out portions until you have a composition that appeals to you. Then mount the secondary picture on white board, and glue on the top picture. The result is a picture in which you view one image through another.

Designs and Decorations
Scrap Timber Assemblage

The assemblage shown opposite is a cheerful composition of wood scraps, with some movable parts that let you re-design it at will. I used a 13 mm thick, 90 cm piece of plywood as the "canvas" for the composition, a 90 by 90 cm length of 13 mm dowel to peg the movable pieces to the plywood, wood drapery rings, wood spools and balls, fabric dyes, rubber gloves, tongs, newspapers, bottle of white glue, half a litre of white enamel, a 5 cm brush, fretsaw, drill with 13 mm bit, medium sandpaper, and a large cooking pot.

To make the plywood mounting board more interesting, a free-form design was traced on one side and sawn out with a fretsaw, as in photograph 5. Then the rough edges were sanded, and it was painted with white enamel. Next, I sanded a random selection of wood scraps in varying sizes and shapes, as in photograph 6, and dyed them different colours, photograph 7.

With the plywood laid flat, I tried various shapes and combinations of wood scraps, drapery rings, pegs, and wood balls, (photograph 8) until I found a basic, balanced composition. The next decision was which pieces should be glued to the board to form a basic design, which should be movable, and which should be glued together, photograph 9. Then 13 mm holes for pegs were drilled into the board and half way into, or all the way through,

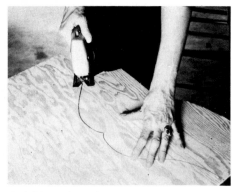

5: A fretsaw is used to cut out a decorative free-form curve. This will relieve mounting board's squared-off look.

6: All wood scraps are sanded to remove roughness, then sorted into groups according to the colours they will be dyed.

7: An envelope of dye is stirred into 4 or 5 litres of boiling water. With tongs each scrap is dipped for a minute.

8: With the mounting board flat, mixtures of shapes and colours are tried until a pleasing arrangement appears. Then it is decided which parts will be fixed, which movable.

the backs of the movable pieces. From the dowel, I cut several pegs, varying the lengths to fit the number of wood scraps that would hang on each peg. The pegs were dyed in colours that seemed right for their places in the composition. Then the basic design pieces were glued to the board and the pegs into their holes in the plywood. With the movable pieces in a pleasing arrangement on the pegs, the assemblage is complete.

9 : Scraps that are glued together should have enough contact area to make a strong joint and not be too heavy for the peg.

10 : A drill with 13 mm bit makes peg holes. Hold wood firmly or clamp in a vice. Most holes are drilled half way through.

With the basic elements glued in place, and pegs for movable parts fixed to the "canvas", the composition awaits the artist's final decisions. The pieces at the foot of the "canvas" belong on the pegs: where would you put them?

Designs and Decorations
Cigar box Assemblage

by William Accorsi

The assemblage on the right is probably the busiest cigar box you have ever seen. The box is mounted on the wall with its lid hanging down, and it overflows with activity. A china doll presides as a kind of master of ceremonies, with one arm outstretched towards the time (half past eight) and the other towards the keys. Many faces look out at you, yet who could decipher what is behind their expressions? Indeed, like an unlocked trunk, the box shows you its contents, but you are left to guess at its boundless secrets.

The idea of using a cigar box as a background is excellent, because a box provides a ready-made framework within which to work. The arrangement of matchboxes and pictures supports the illusion of many compartments. At the same time, compartmental boundaries are exploded by the wild mixture of shapes, colours, and the cluster of pieces from a child's game around the top.

You can adapt your own objects to such a cigar-box assemblage. The construction is primarily a matter of glueing them to the box and its lid, after you have worked out the design. Experiment with arrangements until you have the effect you want. Then glue the larger pieces and start fitting

11: Trim ice lolly sticks with pincers or a sharp knife to make frames for small pictures or create divisions.

12: Pictures should be glued in place first and frame parts added last, after the final composition has been determined.

13: Putting an assemblage together. Begin with the larger pieces, to lay out on the basic composition. Small details are added last.

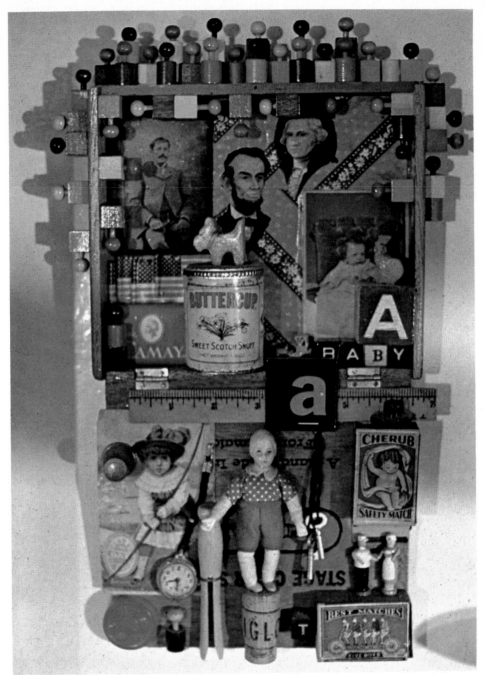

14: A good composition is the key to a successful assemblage. Before glueing, try several variations of your arrangement.

A sophisticated assemblage, constructed in a wooden cigar box, emanates an atmosphere of memories, enhanced by the inclusion of childhood treasures.

the smaller pieces in place. If you want to add frames to small pictures, glue the picture to the box or its lid first with white glue, then cut the parts for the frames from ice-lolly sticks, and glue them into place.

Other possibilities include mounting several odd-shaped small boxes on a board and filling the boxes with objects. Sturdy cardboard gift boxes can be sprayed with enamel paint and used this way. For an assemblage with many small compartments, consider painted tart trays mounted in clusters. A small item such as a marble, shell or stone may be glued in each cup, making every object individually important. String, dipped in liquid starch and dried, provides sturdy partitions when glued on a backing to outline areas. Emphasise by pasting in brilliant papers or fabrics.

Designs and Decorations
Free-form Assemblages

by John Myracle
The assemblages here illustrate something of the effects and relationships of objects within a sculptural composition. The two on this page were developed after contemplation of old printer's type made of wood and the dismantled parts of an ancient clock.

Printer's type assemblages
The free-standing assemblage at left below almost makes you believe that the alphabet continues into the core of the construction; it evokes the atmosphere of old printing houses. Massiveness, greyed colours, and something of the labour of putting hand type together are communicated to us through the weight and precision of the letters on their blocks of wood. Big letters juxtaposed with smaller ones make the composition dynamic and portentous, giving balance and pace to the design.

In the assemblage below, weathered wood and clock parts, added to old

15: Free-form assemblage of old printer's type is supported on a piece of 5 by 10 cm cut wood, so one side is 12.5 cm long, the other 7.5 cm, and joined to the base, a letter "U", by a length of 10 mm dowel, fitted and glued into a drilled socket. The other letters were glued to the wood with epoxy cement.

Framed assemblage adds clock parts and weathered wood to old printer's display type to conjure up an atmosphere that communicates an awareness of the passage of time. The black frame for the composition is 6 mm by 6 cm lath and the background is weathered boarding. The overall size is 40 by 85 cm.

"Dagwood" sandwich is made of kitchen sponges of varying thickness and coarseness. Bread, with edges browned with water colour, is filled with any food the imagination can turn a sponge into: Onion rings, for instance, are painted rolled sponges, sliced crosswise; the egg slices were made in similar fashion. Sponges were rolled after painting, pinned in place with toothpicks until dry, then sliced.

Craftsman's apprentice at work, circa 1791.

printers' type, suggest the relentless tick of time, the ever-present deadlines faced by printers and editors. You can almost hear the clacking of the presses. To make the structure balance, the clock face is off-centre to the left; numbers are staggered to the right in a graceful curve, springs and wheels are set at random as counterpoint to the other elements. Overlap is created by attaching parts with nails of differing lengths.

Exercise in sponges
The sandwich above is a structural assemblage in a lighter mood. This 'Dagwood' special was made from whole or sliced sponges, of varying sizes and coarseness to resemble the size and forms of common sandwich food. Only the lettuce is not a sponge; it is made of crinkled green plastic packing paper. Water colours, white glue, and toothpicks (to hold wet sponges in place as they dried in shape) were the only other materials used to make the sandwich.

This type of art may not be your favourite, but it is fun, and it frees the imagination to seek new forms and ideas in commonplace household objects.

93

COLONIAL CRAFTS
Life in Early America

by Melissa Schnirring

Many of today's hobbies and crafts which are practised for pleasure, originated as part of the daily work of our ancestors. Modern technology may have removed the necessity for most of those crafts, but there is still a great satisfaction in personally creating a beautiful object or an efficient implement, using inexpensive natural materials. The people of different countries, each with their own needs, evolved unique crafts; but the crafts of several countries were combined by the Colonial Americans, nearly 200 years ago. To the knowledge they and their forbears brought with them, they added completely new techniques for making the most of the new country, climate, flora and fauna with which they lived.

Many crafts that we take up today for recreation filled basic needs for the villager-farmer of rural New England in the late 18th and early 19th century. A combination of factors left only do-it-yourself or do-without-it alternatives: the isolation often imposed by primitive roads and rough winters, the subsistence (rather than cash crop) farming in remote areas, and the shortage of cash to buy ready-made articles when they were available. It is not easy for today's do-it-yourselfer to grasp the gravity of these alternatives. Sound crafts knowledge made the difference between comfort and bare existence: if you wanted your hands warm during the icy winters, you had to master all the crafts involved in transforming dirty, tangled fleece on a sheep into finished mittens—shearing, carding, spinning, dyeing and knitting.

The New England farmer and his family responded resourcefully to the challenge. They became skilled at making the articles they needed, using the materials nature provided. Their land was forested, and the trees provided fuel for heating and cooking as well as timber for buildings, wagons, furniture, barrels, spinning wheels and many other farm and household implements. Trees enriched the family diet by yielding nuts, fruits (for cider and pickling, too) and maple sap for syrup and sugar.

In those days the land provided crops that fed the people and their livestock. The livestock in turn gave not only meat, milk, butter and cheese, but wool for clothing, hides for breeches, aprons, caps, boots, buckets, saddles and even drinking mugs; bones for implements; and tallow and grease for candles and soap. The land also furnished herbs for seasoning, flax for clothing, clay for pottery, flowers, leaves, roots, minerals, insects, used for dyeing yarns.

The early New Englander's awareness of nature's bounty and his skill in using it effectively are attributes that we might well envy today. On the following pages is described a way of life in which crafts played a vital role, filling man's need for both comfort and creativity. That is, essentially, what *The Family Creative Workshop* is all about. Many of these early crafts are among the *Workshop's* entries.

Clothing: Re-enacting life early in the 19th century, this Old Sturbridge Village couple are dressed in Sunday best, ready to attend church or a town meeting. Most of such clothing was home-made from raw materials prepared by the family. Some items, such as the gentleman's hat, could be bought only in city shops, and were lifelong treasured possessions.

Maple Sugaring: As it was practised by New England Colonial farmers, maple sugaring is part of the seasonal round in Old Sturbridge Village, Sturbridge, Massachusetts, a museum town that recreates village life in the early days of America. Snow was still on the ground when this first crop of the year, maple sap, was harvested during the early thaws. Note the hollowed logs used to catch the drips, an Indian trick the Colonists learned in the days when buckets were a luxury.

We have chosen to describe crafts of the period between 1790 and 1840. To evoke scenes from rural America of those years, we took photographs in Old Sturbridge Village, Sturbridge, Massachusetts. The Village, open to the public, recreates village and farm life of this period. Its inhabitants are all trained in the early farming and craft techniques.

A look into the past

As the first half-century of the Republic unfolded, the typical rural New England family was an industrious, nearly self-sufficient unit. Of its three main pre-occupations (food, clothing and housing), only clothing was not governed by the seasons. Cloth making was a year-round craft.

Farm life was hard on clothes, almost all of which had to be made at home. A torn garment meant, for a woman, one more mending chore that night by the light of the fire; or by a burning pine or hemlock knot, or tow-wick candle. Nothing that could be repaired was ever discarded. What was worn out became part of something else—an appliquéd quilt or a braided rug, for instance, or a patchwork cushion. The constant need for production did not keep the women from adding touches of grace to their needlework. While not a scrap of cloth could be wasted, simple patchwork, plain or appliquéd, gradually evolved into a folk art of extraordinary originality and beauty.

Babies added to the family's need for cloth, but as they grew up, they helped to make it. Girls learned to knit with homespun yarns when they were about four years old, to spin home grown flax into linen thread when they were six. Men, women, and children wove cloth on looms. Boys even took small looms with them when they grazed the sheep, weaving while they watched over the flock. From the wool and linen, the women sewed clothes and produced the quilts, rugs, towels, curtains, napkins, and other articles for the home.

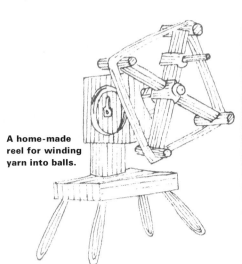

Spinning: A girl spins linen yarn from the long inner fibres of the flax plant, gathered on the spindle on the right. The goal is a smooth, even yarn, twisted for strength. Skill is acquired only after much practice.

A home-made reel for winding yarn into balls.

Weaving: A year-round task for the women was weaving from farm-grown flax, to make cloth for garments and such items as napkins and table runners shown in foreground.

Ploughing: Old Sturbridge Village farmers plough with oxen. Oxen could keep their footing on New England's rocky, rough slopes and on half-drained stubble fields. They were also used for hauling, stump pulling, other heavy work.

The family managed to combine sociability with cloth production. Women took their spinning wheels when they visited neighbours, and they organised the quilting and spinning bees that filled the hours that could be spared from the year's round of farming activities.

Spring

For most of the family's activities, the seasons called the tune in early rural New England. Late winter or early spring, when the sap rose, was the time for making maple syrup and sugar—although a capricious January thaw could send a farmer out through deep snowdrifts to tap his maples. The Indians, whose generosity in helping the early settlers is rarely acknowledged, had taught the farmers to cut V-shaped slashes low on the tree trunks and insert a piece of birch bark in each slash to funnel the sap. The farmers improved on this, if a hand auger was available, by drilling into the trunk and replacing the birch bark with a hollow tube.

Spring was also the time for sheep shearing and much of the planting. New England farms were 20 to 80 hectares in size at this time, but only a small part of this land would be in crops at one time, with perhaps twice as much in meadows or in partly cleared permanent pasture for pigs and cattle. With the primitive implements available around 1800, it was a very hard day's work to plough half a hectare and even slower, backbreaking labour to harvest it. A farmer thought twice before he planted additional land, especially if he did not have a ready market for the surplus—that is, if he did not live near a sizeable town; or at least close to a river, by far the best means of transport in those days.

Maize (Indian corn) was the basic crop and the main foodstuff for farming families and, with hay, for livestock winter feed. Hard work breeds hearty appetites, but our educated palates today would rebel at such an incessant onslaught of corn; corn mush (hasty pudding), boiled corn, roasted corn, corn meal baked into corn cake and corn pudding. A blight of parasites harboured in barberry bushes had wiped out wheat crops by 1800 in all of New England except Vermont and along the western state borders. This meant the virtual disappearance of white bread; the substitute was corn meal and rye flour bread called "rye and Injun".

Churning Butter: It required little skill but lots of elbow grease to keep the wooden handle moving up and down until the butter solidified. Churning was one of the many chores that kept housewives busy throughout the year.

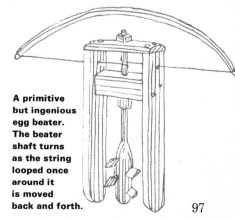

A primitive but ingenious egg beater. The beater shaft turns as the string looped once around it is moved back and forth.

97

As well as corn, the farmer planted hay, with a shade crop of oats, in the spring. The hay would not be ready for harvest until the following year, but the oats would be ready in August. He also planted flax to provide the fibres from which the women spun thread for weaving cloth. Potatoes and the kitchen garden (including most of the vegetables we know today, except for the tomato) went in as soon as the earth warmed, with herbs, destined for the meat stews that would provide some variation from the eternal diet of corn. Throughout the growing season, as each crop ripened, there would be preserving and pickling work for the women and girls, as well as jams to make to stock the larder against winter.

Summer

The frantic pace of the spring planting season eased a little as the weather grew warm. Though there were hay, rye, and oats to be harvested and potatoes to be dug, other jobs sent the family ranging the countryside; and these were more like diversions. Fishing and snaring small animals added to the variety of summer meals. In the hot, lazy days of midsummer, there were berries to gather: first raspberries and wild strawberries, then bilberries. There were sweet-smelling herbs to seek, for scattering on the church benches and for making little dried nosegays to scent drawers and linen stores. Other herbs were medicinal. Many berries, nuts, and tree barks (maple, walnut, and oak) were used for dyeing yarns.

For the farmer, as the kitchen garden grew, there was the pleasure of watching over, tending, harvesting, and drying the seeds of those vegetables that were the best of the year's crop, to provide good seed for the next year's sowing. As the season waxed, then waned, the family began to collect materials for winter crafts—the right piece of wood to carve into a toy, a staircase banister, or a spindle; perhaps special boards to bend and smooth

Haymaking: Lacking mechanical aids, the early American harvested hay for his livestock by hand, using hand-made implements.

A home-made wooden fork for pitching hay

Candle Dipping: Simple but time-consuming, the making of candles by hand was best done outdoors because it was a messy, smelly chore done over an open fire. The number of dips determined the candles' size.

for a cradle for the next baby, rushes for winter basketmaking, a gnarled briar root for a pipe, corn stalks for a new broom.

Summer was the time for home improvement on a large scale. During the early 19th century many rural New Englanders were beginning to turn their log cabins into buildings for livestock, and were constructing frame houses for their families. In very remote areas, they still hewed beams (oak in New York State, maple in Vermont, chestnut elsewhere if it was more plentiful) and sawed the white pine floorboards by hand; but sawmills now began to appear on every New England river. A nail-making machine had been invented, so nails were no longer rare and expensive. After weeks (with a sawmill near by) or months of preparation, neighbours were summoned to help to join and raise the frame for the new house. This was always a festive occasion, with outdoor tables loaded with food and drink prepared by the new home owners for all the helping hands.

All was not unrelieved toil for the farm family, especially as the 19th century progressed. Many of the hard but necessary chores were shared and enjoyed. Group activities were organized for men as well as women—to clear a field of stumps, to raise a house, to augment a farmer's timber supply, and, most popular of all, to husk maize. After a corn-husking, there was always time for athletic contests. Hunting, fishing, skating and swimming were popular all round. There was Training Day with its public shooting matches (later replaced by Independence Day); boisterous Election Day, County Court Day, and the agricultural fairs of the early 1800s.

Autumn

With autumn came the last urgent preparations for the months ahead, when the land would lie still under its winter blanket, and warmth and food would depend on the industry and wisdom of the preceding seasons. There was corn to be harvested, rye for the following year to be sown. The last of the fruits and vegetables had to be picked and stored, dried or pickled, or preserved.

The men did the heaviest work, but for the women it was a time of almost frenzied activity. The autumn apples had to be sliced and hung on long strings from the rafters to dry; or stored in barrels in the cellar, straw separating the layers to prevent one bad apple from spoiling the lot. The last of the garden crops were stored—potatoes, turnips, onions, beet, cabbage, parsnips, carrots, squash, pumpkins, pears, whatever would keep.

Autumn brought butchering time, and for a few weeks there was fresh meat. For future use most of it had to be pickled in brine, though some of it was smoked or dried. Animal fat was rendered into tallow for candles, which had to be made outdoors. The women worked long hours to prepare a good supply while the fair weather lasted—and was followed by an Indian summer, if they were fortunate. They slip-knotted candlewicks on to candle rods, dipped them and cooled them alternately as many as 40 times, heating the tallow in a large iron cauldron over an open fire. They also used animal fat for soap making, combining it with lye from leached ashes. Some dyeing had to be done in the autumn: yellow from goldenrod or onions, for example.

Using flails the men threshed the harvested rye on the barn floor, separating the grain from the straw; then winnowed it outdoors in a shallow bowl, tossing the grain in the air so the wind could blow away the chaff. Corn for the livestock was cut and stored in September. Corn intended for human consumption was tied in bunches or stooks and left in the fields to dry and harden. Later on, some of it was brought in, husked, shelled (in some cases with a flail, but usually with a knife or crank-operated corn sheller) and taken to the nearest mill for grinding into corn meal. Some stooks were left in the fields until needed in winter.

Winter

Once the snows of winter had locked in the last pasture, important indoor tasks were waiting. Cloth had to be woven. There were tools, implements,

Broom making: With the aid of this primitive but efficient binding machine, the broom maker could produce ten or twelve sturdy brooms in an hour.

A Colonial broom made of corn stalks.

and furniture to be made or repaired. Boots and shoes had to be mended—more likely the former, for the winter soil held moisture like a sponge, and the farmer almost always wore boots. Harnesses were mended, and cracked or broken pottery was mended with linen thread. As spring approached, corn was husked and shelled; the best ears, with the straightest rows of kernels, were set aside for planting; and grain was threshed for spring sowing.

The farming family was by no means locked in by winter. The snows smoothed the primitive roads and made sleighing parties feasible; trips to town were easier (some townspeople used rollers to pack down the road snow); and visits to distant friends were possible. Families packed and came to stay for days and perhaps for weeks, catching up on all that had happened since the previous year. Even if they stayed at home, there was time during the frozen months for a man to carve a briar pipe, for a woman to cross-stitch a sampler, for a daughter to add to her bottom drawer.

The snow also opened the way for a vital winter job—getting in firewood

Blacksmithing: A Colonial blacksmith's shop includes a lever-operated, overhead bellows, and the wide variety of tongs and other tools needed for forging and tempering metal.

Log splitting: Colonial farmers often split logs for board-making, but they took advantage of riverside sawmills to cut wood for houses, barns, fences, tools, and furniture.

for the year. Farm life required firewood in enormous quantities. The kitchen fireplace or stove was always wood-hungry. In a large house, a fireplace or stove in the kitchen used wood all winter. Dyeing, soap making and the smokehouse consumed a lot of wood in autumn. In season, maple sugaring created a tremendous demand for wood, as the farmer had to boil down 140 to 200 litres of maple sap to get 4.5 litres of maple syrup. With further boiling, he got about 3.6 kilos of maple sugar from 4.5 litres of syrup. In the early 1800s, a 40-hectare farm often produced as much as 450 kilos of sugar a year.

Wood was cut in winter because the task was easier then for both man and beast. The snow cover made hauling lighter because there was less drag on the sleigh runners. (Sleighs were used for year-round hauling, due to the shortage and expense of wheels.) At first, farmers used an axe for cutting wood; later on, a two-man saw, doubtless proving the saying that wood is the fuel that warms you twice, once when you cut it and once when you

Tinsmithing: A tinsmith solders together tin pieces, then forms them with hand tools, just as the Colonists did. Early tinsmiths not only produced table and storage vessels, but mended them.

burn it. Wood splits more easily when frozen; and wood cut when the sap was not running was less prone to insect attack, and more secure for building.

Do-it-yourself and commercial trade

The intense round of seasonal activities on which comfort and even survival depended did not ease as the 19th century progressed; but the New England farmer's means of coping with them did. In 1790, he was quite likely to make his own boots, hammer out spades and two-tined forks on his own anvil, and make whatever new furniture was required. The combined efforts of the men and women produced everything they needed except coffee, tea, spices, molasses, and salt; of these, only salt was indispensable. The local store sold these commodities, as well as more ornate cloth than the women could make from wool and flax. The farmer could pay for his purchases in cash if he had it, or exchange surplus produce: cheeses, grain, flax seed, hides, tallow, timber, pork, beef, wood ashes.

By the turn of the century, however, peddlers began to carry all sorts of wares to the most remote districts. Visits by travelling artisans became frequent enough to replace many chores. such as hide tanning and boot making. As towns grew larger, more specialised shops appeared: a West Indian goods shop, a hardware store, an apothecary's shop, and even a millinery shop. Artisans opened shops: blacksmiths, potters, broom makers, pewterers, coopers, cabinet makers, and tinsmiths, usually part-time farmers themselves.

Basic materials became more plentiful. Iron mines and blast furnaces, up and down the river Connecticut and along the New York-Massachusetts border, were catching up with the demand; by 1812, there were 160 cotton mills in Connecticut, Rhode Island and Massachusetts.

By 1840, the degree of craft-dependent self-sufficiency required for survival had diminished, but some of the crafts continued to flourish. Some of the products of necessity that the New England farming families crafted (exquisitely appliquéd quilts, for example) have not only survived but are on display in museums today.

Pewter making: A pewterer heats a spoon mould over a candle. He will pour in the molten pewter, let it cool, strike it loose, smooth and polish it.

Sheep is placed upright, all four legs extended, to keep it still while it is being sheared. Once seated, animal behaves surprisingly well.

Sheep shearing and wool carding

A review of the early steps in the home production of wool yarns shows some of the effort required in Colonial times to provide raw materials for the craftsman. The process of yarn making begins with sheep shearing, a painless—to the sheep—but messy job. The process has changed little, although today electric shears are used instead of hand shears.

The shearer placed the sheep upright to immobilise it, and began shearing at the neck, working down the underside, then cutting up around the neck and head. So that he could roll the fleece back as he worked, he pulled the fleece apart along the centre of the underside. Working from the underside around to the back, he sheared towards the tail, rolling the fleece back as he went. He was careful not to cut into the roll, which would create shortened, useless fibres. A similar pulling-apart process was also necessary for each leg, but the result was an entire, intact fleece. It took an hour or more to shear a sheep with the hand clippers used around 1800, and by the end, the shearer's clothing was covered with the lanolin from the sheep's skin.

Preparing the wool

The oily wool was cleansed in a large kettle in a mixture of one part urine (urine was one of the few sources of ammonia then) to two parts water. After being rinsed and dried, it was ready for carding.

In Colonial villages, carding was done by hand, at home. The wool had to be picked over to remove dirt, burrs, twigs, and other foreign matter. Then a little oil was added, and the wool was carefully combed or carded by hand with wooden cards, implements that look like wire brushes. (These can be bought today at craft and hobby shops.) Using two cards, the carder opened the wool fibres and then drew them together, combing the wool from one card to the other, finally forming a roll of fluffy strands (see photograph on opposite page.) The wool fibres were then ready for spinning into yarn and dyeing.

Dyeing the yarn

Before the mid-19th century, basic dyeing was done with such natural materials as dried insects, powdered minerals, roots, flowers, and leaves. When easy-to-use chemical dyes were invented, home-made natural dyes quickly lost popularity. However, a characteristic of natural dyes—the unpredictability of their colour—is exactly what makes them appealing to today's home dyers. They produce individual rather than standardised effects on yarn or fabric. No two dye lots are identical.

Some of the natural dye sources that have been used at one period or another can be found almost anywhere in this country as well as in North

Demonstrating hand shears, the tool used in Colonial times. Today, shearing is done with electric clippers.

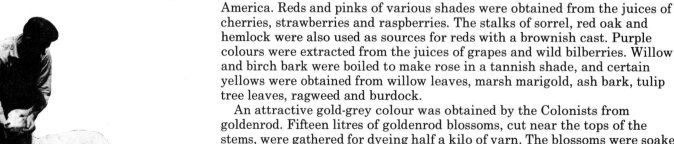

America. Reds and pinks of various shades were obtained from the juices of cherries, strawberries and raspberries. The stalks of sorrel, red oak and hemlock were also used as sources for reds with a brownish cast. Purple colours were extracted from the juices of grapes and wild bilberries. Willow and birch bark were boiled to make rose in a tannish shade, and certain yellows were obtained from willow leaves, marsh marigold, ash bark, tulip tree leaves, ragweed and burdock.

An attractive gold-grey colour was obtained by the Colonists from goldenrod. Fifteen litres of goldenrod blossoms, cut near the tops of the stems, were gathered for dyeing half a kilo of yarn. The blossoms were soaked overnight in water in a large kettle. Next day, they were boiled in water for two hours. After cooling, the mixture was strained through several layers of cheesecloth. On the third day, it was ready to be used for the dye bath.

Other yellow shades were obtained from various flowers and from dried onion skins. More than half of the natural dyes produced yellows. Browns were obtained from black-walnut shells and various barks, rusts from madder and other roots, green-greys from many plants, including lily-of-the-valley leaves and sedges. The indigo peddler supplied the blues.

The first step in the dyeing process was mordanting the spun yarn fibres,

The shorn sheep is rid of its hot coat of wool for the summer. The large, intact fleece will be spread out for sorting.

so that they would combine permanently with the dye, thus fixing the colour. The Colonists used a mixture of potash alum and cream of tartar or, after 1820, a chrome mordant. Two huge kettles were suspended over open fires. One held hot water, in which the yarn was soaked for about an hour; in the other was the warm mordant bath. After soaking, the yarn was transferred to the mordant bath and left for an hour over the fire. Then it was allowed to cool, rinsed in cold water, and hung out to dry.

For the dyeing, one large kettle was filled with water and another with 18 to 22 litres of the strained colour mixture. As in the mordanting process, the yarn was soaked for an hour in hot water; then it was simmered for another hour in the dye bath. Later the yarn was rinsed in cold water and dried.

You can use these same processes today for home dyeing. Pick the dye plants at the peak of their season, as the purest colours are obtained from

Carding: Two cards, each covered with nail-like teeth, were used to work the sheared fleece into long rolls of wool fibres. The process eliminated short, unworkable fibres, and left the others parallel.

Dyeing: Hanks of yarn spun from carded wool were dyed, then hung to dry. Wool dyeing, like candle dipping, was done outdoors because both generated unpleasant smells.

Wool was placed on one card and brushed lightly with the other until spread evenly. Heavier strokes were then used to return it to the other card, and the process was repeated several times.

fresh flowers or plants just as they are reaching maturity. The mordanting and dyeing times and temperatures are also important for purity of colour. Do not use hard water or crowd the yarn in the bath, as this causes the dye to spot and be irregularly distributed. Finally, the dye kettle itself can affect the colours, "saddening" (dulling) or brightening them. Iron kettles tend to dull colours; copper kettles give a bright colour, and brass kettles even brighter. Enamelled kettles do not affect colour.

Dyeing with natural materials produced the subtle earthy tones we associate with paintings of the Colonial period; it is also a fascinating exercise for the modern craftsman. The dyes hold well and rarely fade. Although somewhat unpredictable in tone, the colours are appropriate for homespuns and hand-woven fabrics. Materials for home dyeing are readily available and easily improvised.

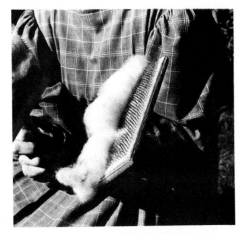

Finally the wool was a light and fluffy roll, ready for spinning into yarn—the next step in the long transition from curly fleece to clothing, blankets and rugs.

The rainbow is created by droplets in the
air which break up white light into its
component colours. It has many more than
the six colours man's vision can detect.
Insects, for example, see colours in the
spectrum that we do not see.

COLOUR PSYCHOLOGY
Rainbow in your Mind

by Louis Cheskin, Stella Blum, Mary Buckley
Colour is a complex and fascinating subject. A visual and emotional cocktail,
it has measurable, predictable effects on man; physiologically,
psychologically, and emotionally. Although we do not know with certainty
why people favour certain colours and colour combinations, the fact that
they do is the basis for a relatively new branch of study called colour
psychology. The term is a loose one covering many kinds of investigation
into man's responses to colour; anything from how to keep him cheerful
in a space capsule, to how to persuade him to buy a tin of coffee.

What colour is

Colour is a two-part (complementary) phenomenon involving the primary colour components in light, or visible energy, and the primary colours in pigment, or matter. If all the colours in light are combined, the result is white light. If all the colours in pigment, or matter, are combined, the result is black, or the absence of light.

Each type (light or pigment) of colour has a set of primary colours. The primaries the physicist works with—the primary colours of visible energy, light—are orange-red, green, and violet-blue. The physicists' secondaries (a combination of two primaries) are the primary colours of pigment, or matter—turquoise-blue, magenta-red, and yellow. The secondary colours of pigment are the primary colours of light. The colour wheel shows these six hues.

What makes colour even more complex is that primaries are not always classified in sets of three. Physiologists and psychologists list four primaries: red, green, yellow, and blue—the ones most people perceive as being independent of the influence of other colours. In colour (process) printing, the pigment primaries are used. In colour photography, the light primaries are involved or implemented as filters in primary colour separation.

You can learn some things about colour. Mix balanced, primary pigment colours to match those on the colour wheel, and you will get black, which is the absence of light. Take three flashlights or projectors; in front of each, put a filter on one of the three light primaries, or physicist's primaries; project all three on to a screen, and the superimposed three will be white.

This colour wheel shows the six basic shades, that the human eye perceives. They are divided into two groups: the physicist's primaries present in white light—orange-red, green, and violet-blue; and the pigment primaries, present in matter—turquoise-blue, magenta-red, and yellow.

Pigment primaries, turquoise-blue, magenta-red and yellow, combine in pairs to form the primaries of light: turquoise-blue and yellow make green; magenta-red and yellow make orange-red; magenta-red and turquoise-blue make violet-blue. All three pigment primaries, combined as shown here, make black.

The power of after-image: Stare at the diamonds for one minute in a bright light; then look at a blank white surface. You should see red and green reversed.

How we see colour

Show five friends the same red, and all will describe differently what they see. Their views are affected by countless factors, ranging from variations in sight to personal and cultural factors. Surrounding conditions—lighting, background colours, and perspective also affect the way you see a colour. Human vision is believed by many scientists to respond to colours in pairs: one pair is black with white, while the others are the psychological primaries, red with green and blue with yellow. That the perception of colour operates at least partly by pairing primaries is indicated by a phenomenon known as after-image. It is illustrated by the diamonds above: Stare at the pair fixedly about 60 seconds; then shift your gaze to a blank white surface. You will see the red and green reversed. The after-image is the part of white light that has not saturated your eyes. If one of a pair of these colours is missing when you look at one colour, your eyes will impose the image of the missing colour if you look away to a white ground.

Dr. Louis Cheskin, Director of the Colour Research Institute of America and one of the early researchers in colour psychology, tells this story illustrating the effects of colour pairing:

He was consulted by a paint manufacturer eager to produce paints in various shades for sale to farmers. The farmers had told him they were tired of traditional farm colours, ox-red and white, and bought them only because they were cheaper than other colours and also durable. Dr. Cheskin advised the paint man to stick to ox-red and white for his farm market, because he believes that red satisfies a "red starvation" incurred from the endless green a farmer lives with in summer, while white has a conditioned association with cleanliness. The paint manufacturer went on with his plans for a range of colours. Eventually he returned to Dr. Cheskin and asked, "How did you know farmers wouldn't buy anything but red and white?"

The fact that we see colours in pairs apparently has other effects. It may account for some of the manifestations of colour blindness. The most common colour blindness is found in red/green perception, and one in 25 men have this to some degree, according to statistics. A man who is severely colour defective in red/green perception sees purple, a combination of red and blue, as grey-blue. He sees greenish-yellow as grey-yellow because his eyes cannot receive the green wavelengths. The colour test shown here is designed to reveal such inherited variances in colour vision.

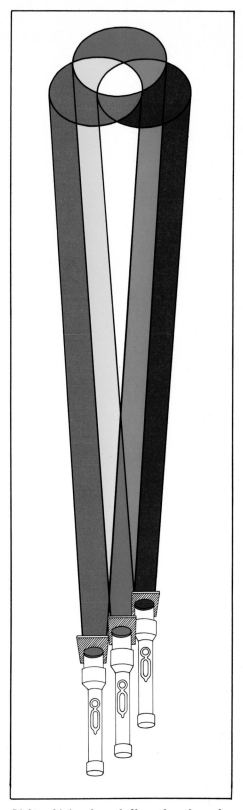

Lights, shining through filters the colour of light primaries, project reflections of the pigment primaries where combinations of the light primaries—orange-red, green and violet-blue—overlap on the screen. Where all three of the light primaries overlap, white light is reflected.

Insects, animals and fish see differently. Most quadrupeds—for example, dogs and cats—are colour blind. They see everything in a grey scale. What angers the bull is the movement of the matador's cloak, not the cloak's red colour. Insects, whose vision equipment differs from ours, are believed to see part of the colour spectrum the human eye cannot see.

Man's response to colour

Man's reaction to colour is both innate and conditioned. Innate responses are those born within us. Conditioned responses are those we have learned. The reasons behind innate responses to colour are still unknown, but we do know that such responses to colour exist. In fact, infants see colour and respond to it before they see shapes. For example, red has great attention-getting power. It is stimulating. Normal children, when presented with a choice of toys of several colours, will choose the red toy.

An experiment conducted by Dr. Cheskin in an effort to measure innate response, placed people (with a medical attendant to measure physiological effects) in rooms of different colours, each totally a psychological primary. The rooms were duplicates in every other way—same exposure to light, same sized walls, same furnishings. In the red room, all large surfaces were red—

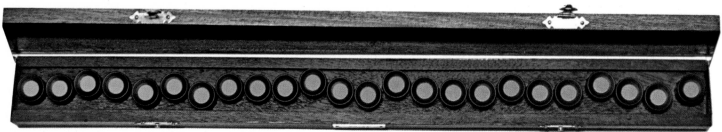

The Farnsworth-Munsell test to define colour blindness consists of sets of coloured buttons arranged in a specific hue sequence from light to dark. The colour-blind cannot correctly reproduce the sequence. The sequence here is one of the four sections of the test.

desks, walls, ceilings, floors, chairs. Some furnishings were of slightly different intensities of red—paper, pencils, other small objects. The other test rooms were exactly the same, but the colours were blue, yellow, and green.

The all-red room, Dr. Cheskin reported, measurably affected the subjects' nervous responses and pulse rate. Many could not stand the red room, could not bear to be in it. The all-blue room caused the pulse to slow and, again, drove many away. The all-yellow room blinded the subjects, and this reaction overshadowed the action of the pulse, which was erratic. No-one could remain in the yellow room for even five minutes. The all-green room caused no physiological reactions, just an eagerness to get away from the intensities of a single colour.

Dr. Cheskin says that doctors and physiologists with whom he discussed the experiment advanced the theory that subjects showed no pulse change in the green room because green is the colour of nature, of growth, of accumulated energy from sunshine and, therefore, man's most comfortable environment.

Conditioned responses to colour

While our need for colour and our responses to the psychological primaries seem to be universal, in effect conditioned reactions and colour associations differ. In Western culture, white is the symbol of purity and black of mourning, while in certain Eastern cultures, white is the symbol of mourning and black of purity.

Conditioned responses to colour result from individual experiences associated with colour and also from exposure to traditional uses of colours as symbols. American Indians used colour to indicate direction. The selection varied from tribe to tribe. The Chippewa used red to represent the east; the Apache used black. The Sioux used blue for north; but to the Creek blue meant south. In Hopi designs, yellow represents the north, green or blue the west, red the south, and white the east.

Ancient Greek colour associations were of a different nature. Blue represented the earth and yellow the air. The Mesopotamians associated protection with colours. They wore blue to avert the evil eye; red amulets to promote healing; blue and violet to preserve faith and virtue; yellow to attract happiness and prosperity; green to induce fertility.

The medieval Catholic Church developed a colour code for the illiterate and even quarrelled with the Greek Orthodox Church about which branch of the church had the right to which colour for which symbol. On statues and in paintings, the Roman Catholic code used red to denote charity, love and martyrdom; yellow for glory and power; green for immortality and faith; pale blue for peace and hope; white for purity; purple for sorrow; black for death.

From such historical uses of colour, coupled with innate responses, we in the West associate red with fire, anger, love, hate; yellow with sunshine and cowardice; blue with calm, peace, depression, stagnation; green with nature, jealousy, inexperience. This colour code is reflected in everyday speech. We talk of seeing red, feeling blue, turning green.

Psychologists see colour as both a key to personality and a tool for expressing or arousing emotions and behaviour. Red is reported to be the choice of out-going, extrovert personalities. It evokes warmth, excitement, rebellion, and strength. It is stimulating, and the presence of warm, red-tinged tones could help to lift your spirits, warm your mood.

Deep blue is believed to denote calm, conformity, passivity, and retreat. Some of its shades seem to have a calming effect; but if you have a tendency to 'the blues', colour psychologists usually recommend that you avoid using much blue in decoration.

Yellow is considered a relaxed, sunny, expansive colour, representing optimism. Its presence in decoration has the cheering effect of sunlight.

Green is widely believed to express eagerness for growth, and to be the most soothing of all the hues for decoration and the easiest to live with.

Man's need for colour

A history of colour in clothing suggests that we have a strong need for, and response to, both established and new colours.

The first dyes were developed when man, having noticed that certain plants, insects, and stones left traces of colour on objects, became skilful in obtaining colouring from natural sources. Ancient Egyptians derived blue pigment from powdered lapis lazuli; Central American Indians prized the cochineal beetle as a source of red; Colonial Americans grew indigo, a plant with blue flowers that yielded a blue dye, as a major crop for export.

So long as dyes depended on hard-to-come-by natural sources, unbleached fibres dominated dress; exotic colours were the privilege of rank and, for a long time, its symbol. The Roman emperors wore robes coloured with Tyrian purple, a valued dye obtained from tiny shellfish. (Emperor Aurelian refused to buy his wife a purple cloak because it was too expensive.) At one time, only China's emperor could wear a particular shade of yellow, the imperial colour. To maintain the coupling of colour with rank in the medieval period, sumptuary laws (those regulating extravagance on religious or moral grounds) restricted the use of colours to certain ranks or professions.

During the reign of Louis XIV, new tints of light blue, violet, yellow, green, grey, and rose were developed. Adopted by his mistress, Madame de Pompadour, the colours influenced all those who came in contact with her; the artists who decorated her salons, the painters who depended on her for their livelihood, and the dressmakers who made her clothes.

With the invention of synthetic dyes in the 19th century, colour became easily available. Fabrics could be dyed strong pinks and blues, magentas, lavenders, and corals, and the new hues were quickly adopted by fashion. Though from then on colour and privilege ceased to be associated, the use of colour has increased with its availability.

CREDIT: SCALA, NEW YORK/FLORENCE

The Emperor Justinian, ruler of Byzantium A.D. 527-565, wears a purple cloak to emphasize his rank in this striking mosaic in San Vitale, Ravenna, Italy. Dye was once so costly that only the rich could afford colourful fabrics. Eventually, purple became the prerogative of the emperor and his family. To wear the purple indicated noble status. The dye came from a shellfish called purpura, found off the coast of Tyre.

Blue distortion of colour plate

Yellow distortion of colour plate

Green distortion of colour plate

Imagine yourself sitting down to a meal tinted like those on the left and you will understand the way in which colour conditioning affects your eye and your appetite. These four pictures simulate an experiment to test the effect of colour on appetite. For the actual experiment, lights were played on the banquet table to colour food in ways that it does not naturally appear.

The photograph above is a reproduction of familiar foods, as close to their natural colours as four-colour printing processes can approximate. The three photographs on the left have been distorted in the printing process to emphasize the blue, yellow and green in the colour plates. To reconstruct a colour photograph with inks printed on paper, as this one is, printers use only four colours—blue, red, yellow, and black—broken up into tiny dots and printed on top of each other in combinations that create the other colours you see here. If you look at this picture through a magnifying glass, you can see the dots of these four basic colours. The printed result represents, but cannot actually duplicate, reality. Your mind, knowing what steak *should* look like, helps you see these dots of ink as steak.

A printer's colour bar, showing the four basic colours at full strength used to print the full-colour reproductions in this book.

Of course, forces other than man's desire for colour are at work in the colour selections of any given era. At the time of the French Revolution, the country's patriotic fervour was expressed by the use of the tricolours of the French flag, red, white, and blue, in home decor and clothing.

How colour psychology is used

Psychologists all over the world have made an effort to disseminate colour tests to co-ordinate information. NASA applied colour psychology to its space programme. The Post Office, car factories, and many department stores, colleges, hospitals, and schools use what is known about colour to convey dignity, authority, and integrity, to boost morale and hence production, to sell goods, to encourage study, to reassure, cheer, comfort.

A colour psychologist's recommendations for a hospital might be like this: to welcome and reassure, halls and entrances painted a warm, gentle apricot or peach; father-to-be waiting rooms in cool greens and blues to calm anxiety; stimulating orange-reds for physical-therapy areas; yellows to create cheer and optimism in convalescent rooms. Pink and peach in operation-recovery rooms reflect a healthy-looking colour to the patient's skin and have a beneficial psychological effect.

Colour association is an aspect of colour psychology subject to much research. Marketing people use colour association to sell products. The food we buy is often colour-keyed—tinted, packaged, or illuminated to appeal to our colour associations. Shoppers transfer the effect of the package to the product in the package. If a food is packaged in a colour not usually associated with that food, it may not be appetizing. Would you be enthusiastic about drinking water that came out of the tap bright green?

In a famous experiment conducted in 1946, a banquet was provided to test colour's effect on appetite. During the banquet, lights that coloured the food strangely were turned on. Many guests suddenly found that they could not eat. Some who continued to eat eventually felt ill. When the lighting returned to normal, appetites also returned.

Sometimes, however, we are protected from such uncomfortable feelings by our colour memory—a habit that lets us see things as we expect to see them, despite changes in lighting conditions. If we own a blue car, for example, we are likely to see that car as blue even under lighting conditions that would make it difficult for anyone else to say what colour it is.

Colour association also affects our sense of taste. It is generally accepted that we can detect only sweet, salt, sour, and bitter flavours, and that the rest of our identification of flavours is associated with our vision and our sense of smell. In another test, consumers were shown coffee in tins of four different colours, asked to smell the contents and to rate them for aroma. Coffee in the blue tin was judged by 79 per cent of those tested as being mild; that in the red tin by 84 per cent as being rich; that in the yellow tin by 97 per cent as being bland; and that in the brown tin by 73 per cent as being strong. The coffee, of course, was identical in all four tins.

Colour psychology and fashion

Colour psychology research in the area of fashion suggests that the keys to colour choice lie in personal vanity and in colour associations. We often choose the colours of the season: in spring, the yellow of sunshine, the greens of sprouting leaves; in summer, flower colours and the light, whitened tints reflected by strong sunlight; in autumn, the browns of fading leaves; in winter, the reddened tones that suggest warmth. And we select colours that flatter our status. Black, often the colour of mourning or of conservatism, as among the Puritans, is periodically re-discovered as a fashionable colour for everything from formal evening wear to expensive lingerie.

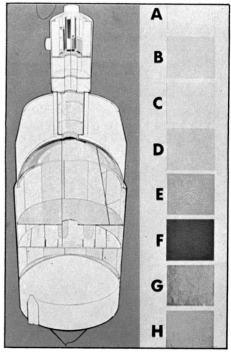

The interior of this lunar module was planned by colour psychologists to use colours selected for beneficial associations as well as for light-reflective qualities and visual relief. The predominantly warm colour scheme is keyed to the psychologically pleasing effect of light on skin tones and food. Since all sections of the capsule are areas in which the crew spent time, work as well as living spaces are colourful.

A. Light yellow: Walls, work area. Door wall, waste- and food-management area. Doors, sleep areas.

B. Yellow-beige: Walls, sleep areas. Doors, food-management area.

C. Light blue: Walls and doors, waste-management area.

D. Medium blue: Beds, sleep area.

E. Orange: Table and chair, food-management area.

F. Bright blue: Handrails.

G. Metallic gold: Floor and wall, grids. Screen vents, outer walls. Dome, upper tank section.

H. Dark yellow: Floors, food- and waste-management areas.

Sweet Tooth Recipes

by Martin K. Hermann

For youngsters, the making of sweets is almost more fun than the eating. Choosing the recipe, measuring the ingredients, licking the whisk are the stuff from which some of the happiest childhood memories are made. True, sweets are low-priority items with the calorie-counting adult; but they are delicious and a good source of energy.

On the following pages, you will find recipes grouped in four categories: Hard Candies, Easy Sweets, Coated Chocolates, and Family Favourites.

Easy Sweets include comfits—fruits preserved or stuffed with various fillings—that require little or no cooking and are suitable for young children to make. Hard Candies, with their high boiling temperatures, are best prepared by adults; but the giant lollipops made with the basic hard-candy formula delight children and are wonderful party gifts.

Family Favourites, which include the fudges and other popular sweets, require varying degrees of skill. The Coated Chocolates are a challenge meant for the experienced cook.

These colourful and mouth-watering confections are all home-made. Clockwise from pink cherry cremes and green mint patties on pedestal stand: peanut brittle in covered glass jar; decorated, tinted lollipops; sugared jellies; almond toffee; rum-walnut bonbons; coconut balls; and boiled sweets. On the centre tray, clockwise from the tinted hard candy: chocolate-almond toffee; chocolate-coated hazelnut-and-raisin clusters in goblet; coconut marshmallow; and assorted chocolates. Recipes are given on the following pages.

Kitchen Favourites and Celebrations
Hard Candies

This giant lemon lollipop is decorated with small sweets, toffee and liquorice.

General procedure

Put sugar, water, and liquid glucose over medium heat, and stir as it heats. When it comes to a full boil for the first time, wash sugar crystals down from the sides of the pot (photograph 1), and add butter or margarine, if called for. Put sugar thermometer in pot, and cook mixture without stirring until proper temperature—146°C—is reached (photograph 2). Remove pot from stove, and add rest of ingredients, except citric acid, which must be folded into cooled batch on baking sheet.

Hard Candy

Basic batch for hard candies:

225 g granulated sugar
60 ml water
85 g liquid glucose

Flavouring of your choice
Food colouring

Follow the general procedure above. Then, from the tip of a teaspoon, drop small bits of hot mixture on to a greased baking sheet, without borders. To sugar-coat the sweets, place cooled pieces on damp towel so they are sticky, but not wet, all over, and roll in granulated sugar. Makes 30 pieces.

For cinnamon and mint drops, add cinnamon or mint flavouring to taste and 8 drops red or green food colouring. For liquorice drops, to the basic recipe add 50 g brown sugar, $\frac{1}{4}$ teaspoon anise flavouring, and 1 teaspoon black treacle. For butterscotch drops, to the basic recipe add 50 g brown sugar, 1 tablespoon butter or margarine, $\frac{1}{2}$ teaspoon salt.

To make lollipops in various sizes, drop cooked hard-candy mix on to tough drinking straws or wooden sticks (photograph 3). Decorate while hot and soft.

Fruit-Flavour Boiled Sweets

For fruit-flavour boiled sweets, citric acid may be added after cooling. This makes the mixture too firm for hard candy drops, and re-heating would destroy the citric acid and make the sweets sticky. Instead of drops, make squares of fruit-flavour hard candy. Use the basic recipe for hard candy, and follow the general procedure above. Add appropriate flavouring and colouring (about 8 drops, yellow for lemon for example), and pour the cooked mixture on to a greased baking sheet. Let cool 2 minutes; then fold in $\frac{1}{4}$ teaspoon citric acid. Fold edges to make batch square. Flatten, and turn over. Score surface, while batch is still soft, with greased edge of a knife. Let cool; then break into pieces.

For large 'stained-glass panes', do not score or break candy; leave it whole.

1: After boiling hard-candy mix (see recipe above), wash down the sugar that clings to the side of the pot with a small, clean brush dipped in cold water.

2: Heat mix to 146°C. Before this, test accuracy of your thermometer in boiling water. It should read 100°C. If not, adjust cooking temperature accordingly.

3: Drop hard-candy mix on straws or wooden sticks to make lollipops. Decorate while hot and soft. Let stand to cool. Do not cool them in the refrigerator.

Family Favourites

Penuche

750 g light brown sugar	2 tablespoons butter
200 ml single cream	1 teaspoon vanilla essence
2 tablespoons golden syrup	150 g mixed chopped nuts

Combine sugar, cream, and golden syrup in a saucepan. Over medium heat, cook, stirring constantly, to 120°C on sugar thermometer, or until a little of the mixture dropped in cold water forms a soft ball. Remove from heat; drop in butter. Do not stir. Cool to 42°C, or until lukewarm. Add vanilla. Beat until mixture loses its gloss and a small amount dropped from a spoon will hold its shape. Stir in nuts. Pour into lightly buttered 20 by 20 by 5 cm pan. Let cool; then cut into squares.

Chocolate Fudge

350 g granulated sugar	2 tablespoons butter
$\frac{1}{8}$ teaspoon salt	1 teaspoon vanilla essence
150 ml single cream	85 g chopped walnuts
2 squares bitter chocolate, grated	

Cook as for penuche, above. Makes a little more than 500 g.

Almond Toffee

125 g toasted chopped almonds	225 g butter
350 g granulated sugar	$\frac{1}{2}$ teaspoon salt
60 ml water	$\frac{1}{4}$ teaspoon baking soda
110 g golden syrup	

Warm almonds in 80°C oven, and keep warm. Put sugar, water, and golden syrup in pot, and stir over medium heat until mixture boils. Wash sugar crystals down from side of pot (see photograph 1, page 113). Keep boiling. Stir in butter until it is completely melted. Put sugar thermometer into pot, and cook mixture to 148°C; stir constantly. Remove from heat, and add salt, baking soda, and warm almonds. Re-heat 1 minute. Pour on to greased baking sheet, and spread evenly to about 5 mm thick. Score into 2 by 3 cm pieces. Let cool. When batch feels plastic, like caramel, turn it over by running a spatula beneath it. When fully cooled, break along score lines. If you wish, coat on all sides with chocolate (see page 117) and extra 150 g toasted chopped almonds. Cool near open window for a few moments only. Makes 35 to 40 pieces.

Peanut brittle and hazelnut brittle look inviting in a clear-glass bowl. Cashew or Brazil nuts can also be used. (Brittle recipe is on the opposite page.)

4: With a knife, score almond toffee into 1 by 2 cm rectangles. Let it stand at room temperature to cool. Do not refrigerate; it would get sticky.

5: After almond toffee has been broken into pieces, it may be dipped into a pot of tempered chocolate and then rolled in a tray of toasted chopped almonds.

Pieces of marshmallow rolled in toasted coconut and coated with chocolate. On this page
is the recipe for Rocky Road, another marshmallow confection.

Hazelnut or Peanut Brittle

250 g granulated sugar
60 ml water
85 g golden syrup
2 tablespoons butter or margarine

65 to 85 g raw hazelnuts or raw
   shelled peanuts
$\frac{1}{2}$ teaspoon salt
$\frac{1}{4}$ teaspoon baking soda
$\frac{1}{4}$ teaspoon vanilla essence

Put sugar, water, and syrup in saucepan; stir over medium heat until it boils.
With wooden spoon, scrape sugar crystals down from side of pot. Stir in
butter. Cook to 136°C on sugar thermometer, without further stirring. Then
stir in nuts, and cook, stirring gently with thermometer, to 154°C. Remove
from heat. Add salt, baking soda, and vanilla. Spread on greased baking
sheet. Cool slightly; then turn it over with a long knife, and stretch it as
thin as possible. Cool at room temperature until hard and brittle. Break into
pieces, and store in container to keep out moisture. Makes 35 to 40 pieces.

Rocky Road

1 batch marshmallow
60 g flour, sifted

675 g coating chocolate
60 g chopped walnuts

Make marshmallow (page 116) without coconut. Cover batch in pan with
flour, and roll in flour instead of coconut. Brush off excess; let dry 2 hours.
Melt chocolate (page 117); gently stir in marshmallow and nuts. Pour into
20 by 20 cm baking pan lined with greaseproof paper or foil; spread about
3 cm thick. Cool. Cut off any to be eaten soon. Wrap rest in foil; it will stay
fresh for weeks.

6: Sprinkle 50 g toasted coconut over the marshmallow. Let it set for 2 hours or overnight in a cool place.

7: Remove cooled marshmallow, with paper, from pan, and cut into squares. Dip knife in water to prevent sticking.

8: Soften the brown paper with a wet cloth, and peel it from the underside of the cut marshmallow squares.

Kitchen Favourites and Celebrations
Easy Sweets

Toasted-Coconut Marshmallow

2 packages unflavoured gelatin	$\frac{1}{2}$ teaspoon cream of tartar
170 ml cold water	$\frac{1}{2}$ to 1 teaspoon vanilla essence
280 g granulated sugar	200 g toasted desiccated coconut

Boil sugar and gelatin and water about 2 minutes, until both have dissolved. Wash down side of saucepan, as when making hard candy (photograph 1, page 113), and bring to a boil. Pour this sugar syrup into a slightly warmed bowl. Add cream of tartar and mix well. Beat at medium speed of electric beater until batch holds a good peak. When it rises over beaters, lift them a little so the tops show (this admits more air), and continue beating about 20 minutes. Stir in vanilla. Pour into brown-paper-lined, 20 by 30 by 5 cm baking pan; spread smooth to about 3 cm thick. For finishing, follow photographs 6 to 9.

Easy Sweets Basic Batch

2 egg whites	1 to 1.25 kg sifted icing
140 ml sweetened condensed milk	sugar

Pour egg whites and milk into bowl; stir with wooden spoon while adding sugar gradually. If it gets too stiff to stir, put on sheet of waxed paper, and knead in rest of sugar. Should be like firm dough.

Coconut Balls

340 g Easy Sweets Basic Batch	1 teaspoon creamed coconut
50 g desiccated coconut	1 teaspoon vanilla essence

Knead all ingredients, reserving 40 g coconut. Roll into a rope, and slice into 2.5 cm pieces. Roll into balls in moistened hands; roll balls in reserved coconut on small plate. Makes 24 to 30.

Mint Patties

340 g Easy Sweets Basic Batch	4 drops green food colouring
$\frac{1}{4}$ teaspoon peppermint oil	

Knead ingredients together. Roll into rope, and cut into 2.5 cm slices. Gently press into patties 5 mm thick. Makes 35 to 40.

Cherry Crèmes

340 g Easy Sweets Basic Batch	4 drops pink food colouring
$\frac{1}{4}$ teaspoon citric acid, or 1	10 glacé cherries, halved
teaspoon lemon juice	10 glacé cherries, chopped

Knead all ingredients except cherries. Roll into rope; cut into 2.5 cm slices. Round these, and flatten slightly. Top each with cherry half. Makes 35 to 40.

Fruit Comfits

To make candied peel comfits: prepare orange or lemon peel by cutting lengthways. Cover in cold water, bring to boil and cook slowly about 15 minutes, until soft. Drain, scrape out white pith, and cut in thin strips. Boil 225 g sugar and 110 ml water, then add 150 g prepared peel. Cook slowly until peel is almost transparent (about 112°C). Take out peel, cool, roll in granulated sugar, and spread on greaseproof paper to dry. To make stuffed-date comfits: Soak dried dates in orange juice, or rum. Remove stones. Fill each with marshmallow or walnut half. Roll in icing sugar.

9: Pull apart squares, and roll in the 150 g coconut. Dry for 2 hours; then store in covered jar or cellophane bag.

Kitchen Favourites and Celebrations
Coated Chocolates

Making coated chocolates is challenging and fun. Centres suitable for coating are toffee squares, nougat, fudge, marshmallow, fondant or mint crèmes, nuts, raisins or crystallised fruits. To coat 500 g of centres such as toffee, I work with 1 kilo of chocolate. But 250 g of chocolate will coat 250 g of small pieces such as peanuts or raisins.

Chocolate for coating is available from specialist suppliers, usually by mail order: one such supplier is Baker Smith (Cake Decorators), 65 The Street, Tongham, Farnham, Surrey. This chocolate, often called 'dipping chocolate', is available in light and dark colours and does not need tempering. Store in a cool dry place, but not the refrigerator. Chocolate flavour cake covering can also be used.

Melt 500 g of dipping chocolate, cut in small pieces, in the top of a double boiler over hot water. Do not let steam or water contact the chocolate, or let the top pan actually touch the water. Bring water to the boil, remove the pan and allow the chocolate to melt, stirring until it is melted and quite smooth. The chocolate can be re-heated gently at any time and fresh chocolate can be added to that in the pan.

A dipping fork makes chocolate coating easier but if one is not available, make an alternative from thick wire, about 25 cm long, with a 1 cm loop on the end. Place the chocolates on waxed or non-stick paper; never oil or dampen the surface on which the chocolates are placed.

During dipping the chocolate should be kept at about 35°C, almost cold to the touch. If it is too hot, the finished result will be streaky and dull. The water in the bottom of the double boiler should be about 40°C. Submerge the centre to be coated completely in the chocolate, and lift out with the dipping fork or a small palette knife. Tap fork or knife gently against the edge of the pan and smooth off surplus chocolate with a skewer. Slide the chocolate gently on to waxed paper. Decorations can be added at this stage while the chocolate is soft, or secured later with a dab of liquid chocolate.

To make nut and raisin clusters, mix 250 g chopped nuts and seedless raisins with 250 g melted chocolate. Spoon small clusters on to waxed paper or into paper or metal sweet cases. Cool at room temperature.

10: Spread liquid chocolate on a non-stick baking sheet to make chocolate squares. Mark shapes before it sets.

11: Use two spoons to move nut clusters from the coating chocolate on to a sheet of waxed paper.

Home-made chocolate-coated candied ginger and nut clusters look just like those you buy—but always seem to taste better.

117

Here are some simple but delicious
ideas for decorating home-made chocolates.
The fillings include fudge, nougat,
peppermint crème, crystallised pineapple,
nuts and raisins; they are decorated
with crystallised violet and rose petals,
hazelnuts, walnuts and pistachios, and
different patterns of dark and light
chocolate. You will have fun inventing
118   your own designs and decorations.

COSMETICS

Making your own Make-up

by Marcia Donnan

The cosmetician is often regarded as something of a sorcerer. But the truth about cosmetics, even expensive ones, is that there are few mysteries in their production. Reasonable substitutes for many products can be made safely and economically at home. As a matter of fact, some of the best cosmetics manufacturers began with just a recipe, ingredients, a large pan, and a kitchen stove.

On the next pages are formulas for such basic cosmetic products as cold cream, vanishing cream, skin freshener, and simple powders. The chemical ingredients used are sold by most pharmacists. These products are made with ingredients that time and usage have proved are safe for all but the most unusual of skins.

Although the measurements used here have been converted from laboratory specifications into standard kitchen-utensil terms, these basic formulas are well established in the cosmetic industry. Remember as you proceed that you are following scientific formulas, not cookery book recipes in which you can sometimes substitute ingredients or modify quantities. Be sure that you follow the instructions carefully, making no changes. Each formula has been tested carefully and must be followed precisely.

Try those cosmetics that are most used by you and your family. You will be astonished at the economies involved. As you become proficient at cooking up glamour aids, you may want to mix batches as gifts for your friends.

Sugar thermometer, saucepans and a kitchen range are the essential tools for making cosmetics.

◄ A mortar and pestle are helpful in turning out home-made equivalents of fine cosmetic preparations (see page 126).

Fragrances and Distillations
Cold Creams

The following three cosmetic formulas have been reviewed by a prominent dermatologist who confirms that there is nothing in these recipes to cause injury to the average person using them. They should be considered safe for general use, but if you have an unusual skin condition, consult your doctor first. The formula below is for cold cream. Study the photographs and illustrations for tips on measuring ingredients and making cosmetics.

Basic Cold Cream

100 ml liquid paraffin
2 tablespoons plus 1 teaspoon grated beeswax

$\frac{2}{3}$ of $\frac{1}{4}$ teaspoon borax (see photograph 3)
60 ml distilled water
1 teaspoon perfume (optional)

Measure paraffin and beeswax, as in photographs 1 and 2, in a medium-sized container. Combine. Place beaker in a small, deep saucepan, in 2.5 cm of water. Over moderate heat bring water to a boil. Lower heat to prevent burning or smoking. Stir occasionally until wax is melted. In another beaker, dissolve borax in distilled water. Place the beaker in a separate pan holding about 2.5 cm of water and heat the borax solution until it just boils.

Remove from heat. Pour borax solution in a thin stream into paraffin mixture, stirring vigorously (see photograph 4) until temperature drops to 60°C. Add perfume if desired. Continue stirring until mixture is fluffy.

Figure A: Implements necessary to make cosmetics are found in most kitchens: spatula, or broad, flat knife; saucepan small enough to give depth and another large enough to contain small one; glass saucer or flat pane of glass for mixing powdered ingredients; mortar and pestle; glass beakers for accurate measuring, or glass measuring cups; sugar thermometer; ordinary grater.

1: Measure liquid paraffin accurately into a measuring cup or beaker. Ratio of liquid paraffin to beeswax determines the consistency of the resulting products.

2: Pack grated beeswax (see figure B) as tightly as possible into the measuring spoon. Be careful not to leave air spaces between the beeswax shavings.

3: Divide $\frac{1}{4}$ teaspoon of borax powder into three equal parts on a piece of stiff paper. Combine two sections to form the required $\frac{2}{3}$ of $\frac{1}{4}$ teaspoon measurement.

4: Use thermometer as a stirring rod when stirring emulsions. This makes it easy to keep an eye on critical temperatures as you are working.

As a rule, commercial vanishing creams are light, soap-based creams made by suspending oil in water. Less oily than most cold creams, the vanishing cream below which contains no soap seems to disappear into the skin almost immediately upon application. Its moisturising qualities are ideal for any skin type. Because of its light texture, it can be used under a liquid foundation or face powder as an all-day protective base.

Basic Vanishing Cream

100 g stearic-acid powder
½ teaspoon potassium carbonate
25 ml glycerine

240 ml distilled water
1 teaspoon perfume (optional)

Place stearic-acid powder in a beaker in a saucepan holding 2.5 cm of water. Heat very gently until powdered acid liquefies. In another beaker, combine potassium carbonate, glycerine, and distilled water and heat in the same manner. When mixture reaches the boiling point, remove both saucepans with beakers from heat. Stirring constantly, pour the glycerine-water solution in a thin stream into the liquid stearic acid. Slowly stir mixture with a spatula until the carbon-dioxide bubbles stop rising. Remove beaker from pan, and with thermometer as stirring rod, continue stirring briskly until temperature of cream drops to 57°C. Add perfume to strength desired, blend it well. Continue stirring until solution cools and becomes creamy—about 15 to 20 minutes. Let stand for several hours, until completely cool. Give mixture a final stir, and pack it into containers.

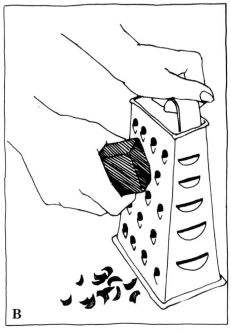

Figure B: To get required amount of beeswax for recipes calling for spoon measurements, rub wax on cheese grater; then press wax chips into measuring spoon.

5: Use a spatula or flat kitchen knife to pack powders like stearic acid into the appropriate measuring cup. Always make certain that your measurements are exact.

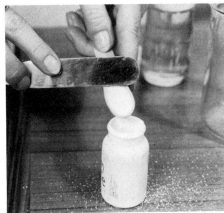

6: Use spatula to level off excess potassium carbonate from the measuring spoon back into the chemical's container. In this way, you save for your next batch.

7: Glycerine, being poured here, is an excellent emulsifying agent. It is one of the basic ingredients used to hold the cream together.

8: Use only distilled water for these formulas. Tap water risks the possibility of introducing foreign matter such as undesirable mineral additives.

9: Stir the ingredients in both beakers until stearic-acid powder in one beaker liquefies and the glycerine solution in the other comes to a boil.

10: Use pot-holders, trivets, or heavy cloths to protect table tops from the heat of saucepans and beakers just removed from boiling water.

11: Pouring one solution into another in a thin stream allows the base to absorb the new ingredients gradually into its chemical structure.

12: Add fragrances, either pure essence or perfume, slowly, drop by drop. Use your own perfume or buy bottled essences from a chemical supply house.

13: Keep testing the final product for thickness. When the stirring rod (as shown here) or spoon is coated with a milky-white cream, the product is in its final stage.

14: What looked like soapy dishwater before its 20 minute stirring becomes a rich, velvety vanishing cream. As the cream cools it also hardens but a brisk stirring before using restores the creamy consistency.

Fragrances and Distillations
Astringent

Astringents are designed to fulfil several cosmetic purposes. Besides the refreshing effect they have, they help to add life to dull-looking skin by whisking away surface dirt left by soaps or cleansing creams. Astringents are ideal for oily skin complexions because they clear away excess skin oils: an abundance of oil can lead to skin problems—for instance, blackheads and pimples.

The word astringent is defined as a substance that draws together or contracts tissue. This action on facial skin is quite salutary, since it brings the tissue to a healthier tone and thus a more attractive appearance.

Although astringents generally do seem to tighten enlarged pores temporarily, no claims are made here. We do know, however, that because of the light, fresh scent included in the following recipe, it acts as a stimulating pick-me-up in hot weather.

Basic Astringent

¼ teaspoon borax
3 tablespoons distilled water

2 teaspoons surgical spirit
3 tablespoons rose water

Combine borax and distilled water in a beaker and place in a narrow pot holding about 2.5 cm of water. Over low heat, stir the mixture constantly until the liquid is clear and all the borax has been dissolved.

Remove beaker from heat, and let stand until the liquid is cool—this will take about 10 minutes. Now add the surgical spirit and rose water, and stir until mixture is well blended.

Do not make any substitutions for ingredients specified.

15: Combining borax and distilled water to form the liquid base of this simple to make, skin-freshening astringent. Be certain that measurements are precise.

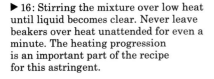

▶ 16: Stirring the mixture over low heat until liquid becomes clear. Never leave beakers over heat unattended for even a minute. The heating progression is an important part of the recipe for this astringent.

17: Adding precise measurement of surgical spirit which acts as a solvent.

18: Adding precise measure of rose water which gives an attractive, light fragrance and refreshes the skin.

Personal Powders

It is very easy and inexpensive to prepare powders with your own personal choice of fragrance. Three basic recipes are given below.

Dusting Powder

Buy 50 g unscented talcum powder (available from chemists) and add about ½ teaspoon of your favourite perfume, or a flower water or cologne to match your range of toilet goods. Mix the perfume in thoroughly, allow to dry, and sift powder through a fine sieve. For a stronger fragrance add a little more perfume, dry, and sift again.

Make sure that powder ingredients are completely blended, and that the texture of the powder is consistently fine and even.

An experienced cosmetics maker always works in a well-lighted area, surrounding herself with the tools and ingredients immediately needed.

Dry Shampoo

Combine 25 g of unscented talcum powder with 100 g of powdered orris root, blending carefully with pestle and mortar. Sprinkle it on greasy hair, leave for five to ten minutes, then brush the hair with a soft brush until the powder has disappeared and the hair is soft and fluffy. This is a good 'emergency' treatment for lank greasy hair, but wash it as usual a day or two later.

Eggshell Powder

A natural face powder can be made with eggshells. Collect a bowl of shells, wash them thoroughly and remove any traces of egg white or skin. Crush in a mortar; sift through a fine sieve, and crush again until the powder is very fine and soft. Add a little perfume or flower water, let dry and sift again. Use brown eggshells for a creamy translucent powder.

CRAFTNOTES ON ENLARGING PATTERNS

Throughout the volumes of The Family Creative Workshop, patterns are reproduced for you to copy. To make a pattern full size, follow the system described here for enlarging the grid imposed on the heart pattern.

The system is really very simple. The small grid in the book must be translated on to a grid with larger squares that you will make; the design (in this case, the heart) will be copied on to this larger grid. The size of the enlarged grid you make will depend on what the pattern is for. For example, for a pillow pattern the grid will have much smaller squares than will a grid for a tablecloth or a bedspread. A gauge is given with each pattern printed. Draw the squares of the large grid you prepare to the size given by this gauge.

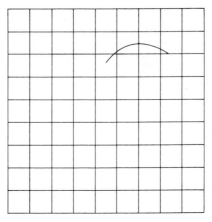

Draw the pattern on to your 6 mm grid, a square at a time.

Above is the pattern of a heart as it might appear in these volumes. The grid placed over it is divided into small squares that actually measure 3 mm. All the patterns in the Creative Workshop use grids of this size. To make a pattern to a 6 mm gauge, transfer the heart pattern on to a grid whose squares are 6 mm in size.

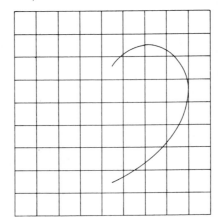

Follow the lines around, checking the book carefully as you draw.

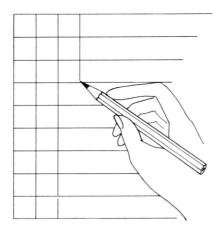

To enlarge the heart pattern, prepare a grid that has the same number of squares as the illustrated grid, but one in which each square measures 6 mm on each side.

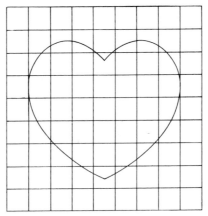

You will find it is easy to transfer the whole pattern using this system.

METRIC CONVERSION CHART

EXACT CONVERSIONS: METRIC TO IMPERIAL

1 gramme=0.035 ounces
1 kilogramme=2.205 pounds
1 millimetre=0.039 inches
1 centimetre=0.394 inches

1 metre=1.094 yards
1 millilitre=0.035 fluid ounces
1 litre=1.76 pints
1 litre=0.22 gallons

OUNCES TO GRAMMES

oz	g	oz	g
$\frac{1}{2}$	14	7	198
$\frac{3}{4}$	21	8	226
1	28	9	255
$1\frac{1}{2}$	42	10	283
$1\frac{3}{4}$	50	11	311
2	56	12	340
3	85	13	368
4	113	14	396
5	141	15	425
6	170	16	453

POUNDS TO KILOGRAMMES

lb	kg	lb	kg
1	0.5	11	5.0
2	0.9	12	5.6
3	1.4	13	5.9
4	1.8	14	6.3
5	2.3	15	6.8
6	2.7	16	7.3
7	3.2	17	7.7
8	3.6	18	8.2
9	4.0	19	8.6
10	4.5	20	9.0

INCHES TO MILLIMETRES

in	mm
$\frac{1}{8}$	3
$\frac{1}{4}$	6
$\frac{3}{8}$	9
$\frac{1}{2}$	12
$\frac{5}{8}$	16
$\frac{3}{4}$	19
$\frac{7}{8}$	22
1	25
2	50
3	75

INCHES TO CENTIMETRES

in	cm	in	cm
1	2.5	11	28.0
2	5.0	12	30.5
3	7.5	13	33.0
4	10.0	14	35.5
5	12.5	15	38.0
6	15.0	16	40.5
7	18.0	17	43.0
8	20.5	18	46.0
9	23.0	19	48.5
10	25.5	20	51.0

YARDS TO METRES

yd	m
$\frac{1}{8}$	0.15
$\frac{1}{4}$	0.25
$\frac{3}{8}$	0.35
$\frac{1}{2}$	0.50
$\frac{5}{8}$	0.60
$\frac{3}{4}$	0.70
$\frac{7}{8}$	0.80
1	0.95
2	1.85
3	2.75

FLUID OUNCES TO MILLILITRES

fl oz	ml	fl oz	ml
1	28	11	312
2	57	12	341
3	85	13	369
4	114	14	398
5	142	15	426
6	171	16	454
7	200	17	483
8	227	18	511
9	256	19	540
10	284	20	568

PINTS TO LITRES

pt	lit
$\frac{1}{4}$	0.1
$\frac{1}{2}$	0.3
1	0.5
2	1.0
3	1.7
4	2.3
5	2.8
6	3.4
7	4.0
8	4.5

GALLONS TO LITRES

gall	lit
1	4.5
2	9.0
3	13.6
4	18.2
5	22.7
6	27.3
7	31.8
8	36.4
9	41.0
10	45.5

(All figures have been rounded off to simplify the tables.)